Praise for *High Performance Business Strategy*

"In High Performance Business Strategy, *Rob van Dijk and Ap Eigenhuis bring together their extensive experience and practical insights from the Hay Group and Unilever into a readily useable work. They offer an elegant yet powerful checklist of questions that build a compelling and thorough HR agenda. Their book is of great value to leaders and HR executives as they seek to create inspired and high performance organizations that engage the hearts, minds and productivity of the human organization."*

Wayne Brockbank, Clinical Professor, Ross School of Business, University of Michigan, and Partner, the RBL Group

"This book offers a specific and useful checklist to help deliver HR value. The nine sections help lay out how to invest in HR to help individuals, teams, and organizations to deliver results. It is a thoughtful guide for action with both good ideas and application of those ideas."

Dave Ulrich, Professor, Ross School of Business, University of Michigan, and Partner, the RBL Group

"The authors have developed an integrated model for managing change. The true value of the model lies in the fact that it has been tested successfully by experienced managers in their day-to-day practice. This book is a welcome addition to management literature."

Harry van de Kraats, HR Director, TomTom

"So many people talk about strategic HR, business partners, HR at the top table and the likes, yet so few offer any insights on how to get there. By combining practical checklists with down to earth business analysis, van Dijk and Eigenhuis manage to deliver what many have been waiting for: the roadmap. Up to you to get on the road or be left watching as others overtake."

Emmanuel Gobillot, author of *The Connected Leader*

"Many of the most important strategic conversations in business today are those that can close the gap between business strategy and talent management. They are the route to sustainable growth and performance through people. The HR function can play a crucial role, and this book sets a powerful agenda for that conversation."

Jonathan Winter, Founder & Director, Ci Group, www.careerinnovation.com

"This book sets out a clear vision for the people side of the business. The approach is business oriented, pragmatic and focused on HR contributions that add value. I recognize some of these from my own past experience and know they work."

Robert Polet, President & CEO, Gucci Group

High Performance Business Strategy

INSPIRING SUCCESS THROUGH
EFFECTIVE HUMAN RESOURCE
MANAGEMENT

High Performance Business Strategy

INSPIRING SUCCESS THROUGH
EFFECTIVE HUMAN RESOURCE
MANAGEMENT

Ap Eigenhuis • Rob van Dijk

**KOGAN
PAGE**

London and Philadelphia

Publisher's note

Every possible effort has been made to ensure that the information contained in this book is accurate at the time of going to press, and the publishers and authors cannot accept responsibility for any errors or omissions, however caused. No responsibility for loss or damage occasioned to any person acting, or refraining from action, as a result of the material in this publication can be accepted by the editor, the publisher or either of the authors.

First published in Great Britain and the United States in 2007 by Kogan Page Limited

120 Pentonville Road
London N1 9JN
United Kingdom
www.kogan-page.co.uk

525 South 4th Street, #241
Philadelphia PA 19147
USA

© Ap Eigenhuis and Rob van Dijk, 2007

The right of Ap Eigenhuis and Rob van Dijk to be identified as the authors of this work has been asserted by them in accordance with the Copyright, Designs and Patents Act 1988.

ISBN-10   0 7494 5013 4
ISBN-13   978 0 7494 5013 7

British Library Cataloguing-in-Publication Data

A CIP record for this book is available from the British Library.

Library of Congress Cataloging-in-Publication Data

Eigenhuis, Ap.
  High performance business strategy : inspiring success through effective human resource management / Ap Eigenhuis and Rob van Dijk
        p. cm.
  Includes index.
  ISBN-13   978-0-7494-5013-7
  ISBN-10   0-7494-5013-4
  1. Employee motivation. 2. Personnel management. 3. Performance standards. I. Dijk, Rob van. II. Title.
  HF5549.5.M63E36 2007
  658.3--dc22

                                                    2007008566

Typeset by Saxon Graphics Ltd, Derby
Printed and bound in Great Britain by MPG Books Ltd, Bodmin, Cornwall

Contents

Part Three: Understanding the checklist to enable dialogue and implementation

Part Four: Future contexts and considerations for business HR

High-performance business strategy and HR

1

High-performance business strategy

Introduction

Your company delivers good products or services and respectable financial results. We assume that you see room for improvement in the current situation and have the ambition to grow and to make the necessary improvements. You want your company to be admired by others and inspiring to work for. We also assume that you are in business for the long term and that you want to build a company with a high-performance business strategy. You want to achieve this in a sustainable manner and with integrity towards all the stakeholders involved. And we assume that you want to maintain or improve the already high quality of your products and services. The issue that remains is: how are you going to get there?

We want to help you to do this by sharing relevant insights in a practical way. Most of this book is based on our own experience and on a checklist we have used. This checklist has proved to work well for teams in many organizations. We have investigated how the key factors on the checklist compared to recent research, and our findings confirmed our belief that those key factors are the differentiating factors between mediocre companies and high-performance companies. Most of those factors relate to what we generally call human resource (HR) management.

Although most business leaders recognize the importance of the people factor, few of them have been successful in using HR effectively, in such a way as to inspire success and to achieve a high-performance business strategy.

Business leaders who believe they can decide the HR priorities without a deeper understanding of the relationship between business strategy, organization and people will find that their organization never becomes a truly high-performing company. HR managers who believe they can determine the HR agenda for any organization largely within the HR function itself will fail to add value to the organization they work for.

In our view, the CEO and the HR leader need to form a natural alliance so that together they manage the balance between keeping the successful core activities of the past, doing away with other, less successful existing activities and building new capabilities for growth and future success.

What is needed more than ever before is a common view on the business HR agenda that needs to be delivered in order for the organization to be successful overall. Rapid change is happening in all sectors of public and corporate life, and the ability to adapt to such change has become of strategic importance. Clarity on what needs to be done on the human side of the organization is vital. In a high-performance company, people behave in an inspired, responsible and decent manner. Such a company has a way of doing business whereby 'heart and mind' come together.

'The New Business HR Agenda'

We want to share with you a deeper understanding of how an inspired performance can be achieved. To help you reach such an understanding, we have developed a checklist through which to generate and agree the new business HR agenda with all key stakeholders in a pragmatic and effective manner. It makes possible a dialogue to clarify what CEOs and other executives expect from the people side of the business and what HR can proactively contribute to support the execution of the business strategy. It helps HR to deliver its promise and add value to the organization by using new insights.

The origin of the checklist, which we call 'The New Business HR Agenda', goes back to the need felt by a team that was leading Unilever's ice cream activities worldwide. This team regularly visited one or several of Unilever's 40 operations worldwide. The team wanted to have an operational tool with which to assess quickly how each of the businesses was doing and what needed to be done first to improve performance. This tool was intended to give a holistic picture, focusing on both people and organization issues. On the way back from a trip to Asia, two members of the team sat together in the plane taking them to Amsterdam and independently made a list of the topics that the checklist should cover. When they compared notes, the similarity was striking, and this resulted in the first version of the checklist, which was structured around four topics:

1. Is there good leadership in place?

2. Are the strategic priorities clear, aligned and consistent?

3. Is the organization well equipped in HR terms to carry out its tasks in line with the priorities?

4. Is there a winning spirit and a track record of delivery and success in the business?

The team leading Unilever's ice cream activities started to apply the checklist during the next visits they made, and their judgements as to how it was working resulted in some changes and additions. Some businesses that were visited used the checklist to make a self-assessment. This self-assessment was then compared with the assessment made by the global team. The global HR team for the Unilever ice cream business further refined the checklist and provided some conceptual background. After attending a presentation by Jim Collins, author of the bestseller *Good to Great: Some aspects of why some companies make the leap and others don't*, some new points were integrated into the checklist. The checklist became part of the HR planning process and was used to identify the priorities for each of the ice cream businesses.

Further validation of the checklist was done with Hay Group, and it was adapted to make it suitable for more generic use in all sorts of organizations. The updated checklist was presented and tried out during international client meetings that Hay Group organized. On several other occasions, including on visits to Austria, Turkey, Spain and Slovenia, the checklist was yet further validated.

One important step was to turn the checklist into a web tool. The web version of the checklist was used at large conferences in various European countries, so that its validity could be tested in different cultural environments. We collected feedback from individual companies that used the checklist for different parts of their organization. We then presented our findings to the international client meeting of Hay Group in Barcelona and received further feedback.

Several times during the above sessions we were challenged to give the checklist a theoretical framework. We have explored various models in an attempt to do so and are confident that it can be done successfully. In essence, these models add another layer to the approach by grouping the checklist topics into a number of clusters. For example, we used what we called the '4C-model', grouping checklist items into one of the following clusters: Clarity, Capabilities, Commitment and Culture. We also used four other clusters: Organization Effectiveness, Quality of People, Performance Management and Culture Development. However, doing this tends to make the clusters more abstract and generic, which does not add to the clarity we are seeking. The risk is that the discussion tends to shift to the more theoretical question of which of the clusters checklist items should be allocated to, rather than focusing on the checklist items themselves.

Therefore, for the purposes of this book we have chosen to stick to the checklist and to focus on explaining its nine sections and the background to the questions. We will use practical illustrations for the individual sections of the checklist. We believe that we will add most value by promoting the practical and holistic use of the well-thought-through checklist.

High-performance business

We also compared the checklist against the annual Fortune global survey of 'the world's most admired companies', conducted by Hay Group. Some of the top companies in the survey can be called high-performance businesses. Interestingly, most of the factors identified as criteria for making companies admired by other businesspeople are reflected in our checklist.

The Fortune World's Most Admired Companies study surveys 16,000 senior executives and directors from a variety of companies, and consults financial analysts, to identify the companies that enjoy the strongest reputations within their industries and across industries. One of the criteria used by the survey is companies' financial soundness.

Nine attributes of reputation are used to evaluate companies and determine the Fortune industry rankings and the overall rankings:

1. quality of products or services;
2. wise use of corporate assets;
3. financial soundness;
4. long-term investment value;
5. ability to attract and retain talented people;
6. quality of management;
7. social responsibility to the community and environment;
8. effectiveness in doing business globally;
9. innovativeness.

The first four of the Fortune attributes focus on what a business successfully delivers in terms of quality of products and services and financial results. Predominantly it is about business performance and results. It is not difficult to see why a company whose goods and services are of poor quality and whose financial performance is poor will not qualify as one of the most admired companies in the world.

The focus of this book is on the people side of the business. We find it fascinating to see that five out of the nine Fortune attributes (points 5–9) are in this area. What this tells us is that the five attributes concerned do make up a substantial part of the factors that, overall, determine the world's most admired companies, and indeed high-performance businesses. Not only are these five factors fully covered by the 'New Business HR Agenda' checklist, but the checklist offers a more extensive and complete range of all relevant business HR best practices. In addition, the checklist makes possible a holistic approach to generating the HR priorities and building the new business HR agenda.

The ability to attract and retain talented people

When it comes to HR best practices, part of the success of the most admired companies stems from the fact that they do not designate the responsibility for developing people as being exclusively the purview of HR. They spread that responsibility across all lines of business and share it with line managers. The percentage of time that managers at these companies report spending on the management and development of people is much higher than the average for all companies, suggesting that an operations-oriented, manager-driven approach to talent management works best. In fact, we are convinced that talent management is one of the core leadership functions, and that it cannot be delegated. For line managers, it means getting in touch with and showing an interest in developing key people.

Jim Collins, co-author of *Built to Last: Successful habits of visionary companies*, notes how people provide the most consistent source of long-term success among the companies he has studied. Products, business models and other aspects of a business are easy to steal, but having the right people is much harder to duplicate.

Companies with a high-performance business strategy recognize the need for managers who are close to talent and better able to spot opportunities and non-traditional career paths for the people they manage. Being hands-on is critical. Do you remember when Jack Welch retired in 2001 from General Electric, after having served as the CEO and chair of GE since 1981, and was succeeded by Jeffrey Immelt? As early as 1994, Immelt's name was already on a list of some 24 candidates to replace Jack Welch on his retirement. The list of candidates was reduced to 8 by 1997 and to 3 by June 2000. Immelt's selection was announced at the end of 2000. Welch retired and Immelt, the youngest of the three internal candidates, took over in September 2001. Not too many companies find themselves with three extraordinary people ready to fill the top job. Typically, high-performance businesses are more confident of their current executive-level teams and high potentials than other companies. Along with that elevated confidence, they have also developed the bench strength to lead their company in the future. On the flip side, it is a known and measured fact that the out-of-pocket, cultural and psychological costs of having to go outside to replace top managers are high, with disruption across the board.

Even with the current move towards 'flattened' organizations, hiring the right people for the right jobs, and then making sure you do the right things to keep them and move them forward in their careers, is critical. In fact, flattened organizational structures mean that smart talent management is even more important than a decade ago, since role requirements have changed and 'managing horizontally' is becoming more the norm.

The global economy is moving very fast. Some critical skill sets today are different from those that will be needed 10 years from now, just as they are different from those of 10 to 20 years ago. Notwithstanding the importance of technical skills, people can be taught technical skills they are lacking. However, to be successful, companies still need capable humans who are thoughtful, who understand how to work with others and who have maturity and emotional intelligence, qualities that are more difficult to develop.

2

How to use the 'New Business HR Agenda' checklist

Introduction

The 'New Business HR Agenda' checklist helps you to identify what is most needed from the HR side in your organization. It gives an indication of aspects that your organization most likely needs to focus on regarding people issues. It makes possible a proper dialogue with the leadership in the organization on HR matters.

The checklist has its roots in the need felt by the leadership team of the Unilever ice cream business to have an operational tool to quickly assess business and find opportunities for improvements. The power of the checklist is that it contains all key factors for developing a new business HR agenda in a comprehensive manner. The checklist builds on the extensive knowledge we have gained over many years. It is supported by various pieces of research that we will use to illustrate our thinking behind the checklist.

The innovative aspect is the bringing together of various practical insights and latest developments into one comprehensive approach. Many management books offer good insights and useful knowledge, but for specialized areas. This normally leads managers to look at the reality from a narrow perspective, ignoring many other aspects that may be relevant too. The content of our book is implicitly based on many such insights and knowledge regarding specialized areas, but avoiding this 'narrowness'. We want to look at the whole picture of what needs to be done on the people side of a business. This is a new approach, and in this respect our book is unique.

By bringing together various insights and latest developments into one checklist and by using one comprehensive approach, we ensure that what needs to be done can be examined in an effective manner. In addition, the high degree of practicality and the business language used ensure that the dialogue around findings will be adding value and will be helping to establish HR as a good partner in business.

In the following chapters we will explain the background for each of the nine sections of the checklist:

Section 1: Energizing leadership to mobilize people

Section 2: Build the team

Section 3: Shared vision and values

Section 4: Strategic framework

Section 5: Aligned and lean organization

Section 6: High-performing empowered teams

Section 7: Coaching: develop yourself and others to win

Section 8: Create a winning organizational climate

Section 9: Deliver results and reward

Each of these sections will be addressed in one of the following chapters, beginning with the questions in the checklist that are relevant for that section. For each section, we will summarize the knowledge and learning that we used. We will give practical examples, illustrate our points with pieces of research and indicate the latest developments in specific HR areas.

Use of the checklist

The 'New Business HR Agenda' checklist can be used in different ways and we would encourage you to find the way that works best for you. We suggest a couple of practical approaches that work. In all cases we assume that the checklist will be used in a dialogue with the key people in the organization you work in:

- identify the 'high-level' HR strategic thrusts in your organization from the headings of the nine sections;

- analyse in more specificity and depth what the key strategies are for each of the HR strategic thrusts identified;

- use the checklist at our website, www.newHRagenda.net.

We will give some further background to each of those approaches. In the practical application of the checklist so far, we have not come across any one 'best approach'. What we have observed is that in particular the specific questions underpinning each of the nine sections of the checklist provide clarity concerning what needs to be done. Only in exceptional cases can organizations answer all questions positively. Almost always, organizations identify at least two or three questions in each section that require further attention, discussion and planning.

Identify strategic thrusts for HR

The headings of the nine sections have been chosen in such a way that they define what an organization needs to do in order to be successful. They set the direction for the organizational capabilities for success. As such, they do not need to be owned by HR *per se*, although in most organizations HR will be the logical owner.

In our experience, boardroom discussions about the HR agenda often start around detailed and specific HR topics. Although not every board member has a well-informed view on marketing or supply-chain issues, every board person does have an opinion on people matters. In itself this is a good starting point for a proper conversation about what needs to be done on the HR side of the organization, but at some time the discussion needs to be elevated to a higher level. For this purpose a prioritization of the nine sections of the checklist can be a very helpful exercise. Each organization has its own stage of development, its own set of key HR issues and its own list of priorities. Clarity and agreement on what they are helps enormously to steer the efforts in the right direction. The earlier in the process of defining the new HR agenda the right priorities are set, the more focus can be applied in the stage of planning more detailed activities.

The identification of the key strategic thrusts in your organization from the nine headings of the sections works well for a 'high-level' approach. The leadership team in Unilever ice cream used this approach to assess the 40 business units in different parts of the world. On the basis of available financial data the performance in terms of business results could be assessed relatively easily, but the need was felt to have a tool to assess the functioning of the human side of the business as well. This was felt to be a good predictor for future success.

After each visit to one or more businesses, the members of the leadership team would independently score each of the nine sections (using the range 1 for minimum to 5 for maximum). The HR person would collect and feed back the outcome to the team. Once a year, or more frequently if required, a total overview for all 40 business units would be drawn up.

Eventually the one-dimensional assessment on the part of the leadership team was extended and a more interactive approach taken. For example, in the case of the Mexican business the board members were individually asked to score themselves against the nine headings of the checklist (between 1 and 5) and to come up with a collective score after discussion with the other board members. The global leadership team did the same and the scores were then compared. Beside many similarities, two clear areas of difference were identified, and the subsequent discussion focused on one of those two areas and actions to be undertaken by the Mexican team.

The language we have chosen for each of the nine sections, or 'strategic thrusts', gives a flavour of what each of them represents. In our experience, every organization will want to use its own individual wording. The process of finding the right words should not be given too much weight, but nor should it be underestimated. Discussions around the wording of the 'strategic thrusts' can reveal the deeper expectations that various members of the team have.

Key strategies for each strategic thrust

After this first step, further analysis is normally needed to define the key strategies and actions for each of the strategic thrusts identified.

For this activity we would recommend having a closer look at the answers for each of the individual questions in the relevant section. For example, suppose that you have decided that developing 'Shared vision and values' is a strategic thrust that requires attention. You may have answered the first four questions under this section of the checklist with a 'yes', but you may have said 'no' to the question about whether you are using surveys to check how well the values are being lived. In this simple example you would surely want to have a proper discussion about the future use of surveys.

It is not only the questions with a negative answer that are of interest. There may be specific areas where you have answered the question(s) in the checklist positively, but you nevertheless want to continue to invest in those areas.

Use the web tool 'The New Business HR Agenda'

The web tool is available at www.newHRagenda.net and has 56 questions underpinning the nine sections. After having completed the questions for your organization, you will be presented with your 'new HR agenda for the next two years', which gives priority areas and relevant actions. Individual use of the checklist in this way is an efficient way to get input concerning your new business HR agenda.

On various occasions we have asked participants at conferences to fill out the checklist for their own organization. In return we have provided them with an overview of the outcome for all individuals. This gives an indication of where each participant's own organization stands compared to other organizations, which can be a useful benchmark.

An approach that we find very useful is based on different individuals in one organization going through the checklist and comparing outcomes. This approach has the advantage that it creates an immediate dialogue around the similarities and differences of outcome.

Case study: use of the web tool in Kappa Packaging

Susanne Coolen attended the Hay Group conference in Barcelona in April 2005. After the conference she sent a short e-mail to her colleagues asking them to go to the website and answer the questions on the checklist. She relates that a number of colleagues responded that same day, and a discussion about the outcomes started almost immediately.

There turned out to be a fair amount of overlap between the outcomes for her various colleagues, but also a number of differences. The overlapping points were common areas of priority. The further discussion was concentrated on the differences, and this revealed some different opinions between the team members. Susanne says that it was important to understand these differences.

She believes that the benefits of the checklist are twofold. First, with the web version of the checklist it is relatively simple for a larger organization to define the HR agenda. Second, the results of the checklist are presented in a concise and understandable manner. The advantage of this approach is that the dialogue about HR priorities is focused and facilitated by the use of a common tool. No time is wasted on long discussions about priorities where agreement already exists; most time is spent on resolving differences of opinion. The other advantage is speed. Using the tool is not time-consuming, and the answers to the 56 questions are given by real people working in a real organization. The first analysis of what is needed on the people side of the organization therefore can be done, as in this Kappa Packaging example, within a matter of days.

3

The new business HR agenda

What business are we in?

What is needed more than ever before is a common view in any organization on the business HR agenda that needs to be delivered in order for the organization to be successful overall. Rapid change is happening in all sectors of public and corporate life, and the capability to adapt to this rapid change is becoming strategically important. Clarity on what needs to be done on the human side of the organization is vital. We believe that a pragmatic way of defining and updating the business HR agenda, and the priority actions and contributions expected from the HR function, can effectively help to steer the performance of any organization in the right direction.

The word 'business' may be misleading for some organizations. We use this term since it describes the world in which we work and in which our ideas for the new business HR agenda were developed. However, what we said in the previous paragraph does not apply only to businesses as such (that is, profit organizations). The same is also true for public organizations, governments, NGOs, etc.

We would not want to exclude any type of organization. Increasingly, non-profit organizations find themselves in a position where 'business' rules and criteria with regard to how they operate and perform are imposed on them. It is in this context that we will use the phrase 'new business HR agenda' for both profit and non-profit organizations.

Any analysis for the development of HR strategy and action plans should start with the question 'What business are we in and what are the critical factors for success?' More than in the past, HR executives need to have not only a full understanding of the business strategy but also a deep knowledge of how the business works, what the key drivers for success are, what organizational capabilities are needed and which are available, etc. In fact, HR executives must position themselves at the forefront when it comes to new business challenges, so that they can swiftly assess what needs to be done on the people side to make things happen. We believe that this dimension of the HR role is as important as handling the consequences of decisions to reorganize or stop activities in other parts of the organization. As we said in Chapter 1, in our view there is a natural alliance between the CEO and the HR executive. Together they need to manage the balance between keeping the successful core of the past, doing away with other, less successful existing activities and building new capabilities for growth and future success.

We argue that a proper definition of the new business HR agenda, identifying how HR will add value to the organization, must have a higher priority than the reshaping and reorganizing of the function itself (shared service centres). The checklist can create a breakthrough in many organizations where the HR function has a perceived lack of time to look closely at strategy.

Many HR executives in the 1990s paid lip service to these ideas, but the results have not lived up to expectations. We need to find a new way forward, one that will deliver more tangible results. The checklist is an important tool to help us do so, but before we use it we should go back to the question posed earlier: 'What business are we in and what are the critical factors for success?'

The answer to this question is normally felt to be simple and straightforward. However, when we were confronted some time ago with some 40 key people from a large international business having to answer this question, it became clear that the reality is not as simple as is assumed and that the question is more difficult to answer than anticipated. It is our conviction that the same is true for many organizations. The answer, though, is vital for the agreement on a HR plan!

So, what business are you in and what are the critical factors for success?

If you are in the ice cream business with 40 operations worldwide, you want the organization to understand the global brands strategy. The Magnum brand has to be treated in a consistent manner around the globe, and there is not much room for reinventing the wheel in individual countries. You want the organization to behave in a disciplined manner.

On the other hand, you want to maintain a simple framework that gives profit and loss (P&L) responsibilities to each of the regions, and within those regions you want to give substantial freedom to individual operations as regards activating the brands in their geographical area. You want your operators to plan and execute local plans with self-confidence and you want them to act fast. You want them, particularly during the summer season, to respond swiftly to opportunities that arise to sell Magnum ice cream in the most appropriate manner.

Assuming that the business strategy is clear, you want the operators in the business to be given quick decisions on proposals and plans for which they need approval from the next level up.

So, in this type of organization you want discipline regarding the brands, you want to keep it simple regarding the operating framework, you want self-confidence for empowered local execution of the strategy and plans, and you want action and decision making to be rapid. This has its implications for the choices to be made regarding business HR activities and priorities. It will be important to define the key factors for success in such an organization, so that the right people can be attracted and recruited. Leadership needs to create the right conditions for an organizational climate where rapidity of action and decision making thrives.

Regarding speed of decision making, we had an interesting discussion with a colleague from Toyota, who made it clear that speedy decision making is not something that Toyota sees as a goal in its own right. Toyota takes an appropriate amount of time to come to a consensus view on what, strategically, needs to be done and then implements the decision fast and in a disciplined manner. Speed for its own sake is more likely to endanger correct decision making than to promote it, in the eyes of Toyota.

This has its implications for the choices to be made regarding business HR activities and priorities. Toyota is an organization that will want to make significant investments to train its workers to produce Toyota cars in the right manner and in the most efficient manner.

The checklist can cope with each of the organizations referred to above, its specific features and critical success factors, and will lead you to the right decision regarding the areas that HR should make its priorities and concentrate its efforts and resources. The specific answer will vary, but this answer will logically flow from the dialogue around the agreed new business HR agenda.

The agenda and HR strategy

Different organizations use different ways to arrive at their HR strategy. Some decide not to use any formal process for HR strategy development, and focus instead on the expected contribution of HR as part of broader business plans or 'strategy into action'.

For example, Nokia makes an interesting distinction between People Strategy, owned by the business, and HR Strategy, which guides the activities of the HR function. This offers the possibility to be explicit under the People Strategy about what sort of human organization Nokia wants to be and wants to have in order to be successful (shared values, leadership principles, people development, employer brand, etc). The HR Strategy focuses on what is expected from the HR function and what needs to be achieved within a certain time-frame.

The checklist does not aim to offer a complete, start-to-finish solution for HR strategy development. Instead, it helps to identify areas that need attention, and it helps to identify the real priorities for the business and for business HR. We always look at what needs to be done in this order: what does the business need and what does business HR need to do in order to help the business to do that successfully?

Also, we always look at what needs to be done with an action orientation rather than with a theoretical mindset. The checklist offers practical insights for you to use, rather than generalized, woolly theories.

This process of identifying what the business needs to do, or needs to do better, and subsequently looking at what business HR is expected to contribute, will normally trigger discussion about the broader strategic thrusts underlying the identified needs and actions. In this way, the process of developing and clarifying the HR strategy is facilitated by the use of the checklist.

We believe that the 'bottom-up' use of the checklist is an effective tool with which to define the one- to two-year business HR agenda. The approach is accurate and defines the business HR agenda in understandable language for all the stakeholders involved.

The original checklist was developed with business partners, and right from the start the language used has been 'business language'. This has helped to create meaningful dialogues with the business on HR and other topics. We do not want to lose this dimension and want to reinforce it by continuing to use the phrase 'business HR'.

What is new?

Business HR will need to clarify the business HR agenda, while reshaping the function itself. This is not easy, but has been done before. If business

HR is unwilling or unable to manage this process successfully, it runs the risk of being marginalized.

This leads to the question of what, then, the key value-adding business HR contributions in the coming years will be. Part of the answer is to say that going through the checklist will help you to identify what the current gaps are and will guide you in the direction of what needs to be done. However, if your ambition is to lead from the front rather than positioning your organization at an average level, this is not good enough.

Some of the things of the past will definitely continue to be on the agenda of business HR. Like organization design and organization development. Or like leadership development and having the right leaders available at the right moment in time and in the right place. Like performance management and providing tools to enhance the performance of individuals and of teams. And like supporting the development of an appropriate culture.

We believe that the differentiating factor for the coming years will be the need to create a higher degree of engagement on the part of employees at all levels in the organization, combined with the concept of organizations doing business successfully but also meaningfully. The latter includes the need for the active, external engagement of businesses and employees with the environment and with the communities they operate in.

In some of the following chapters we will describe how a higher degree of engagement by employees at all levels can be achieved. We believe that in modern organizations people want to do meaningful work. This implies that they need to understand what the organization they work for in essence wants to achieve and that they buy in to this with their 'heart and mind'. It is this combination of 'mind' and 'heart' that is crucial. Too often today the emotional buy-in does not exist or is underdeveloped.

We could therefore say that a higher degree of 'emotional engagement' on the part of employees at all levels is crucial, but we choose simply to talk about 'engagement'. For us it is clear that this includes the emotional dimension.

The combination of, first, an active, external engagement by businesses and employees with the environment and with the communities they operate in, and, second, winning the hearts and minds of employees is a winning formula.

A number of years ago, business HR in North America showed itself to be an early adopter in terms of supporting the huge drive in the late 1990s to maximize shareholder value. This has led to more material wealth for large groups of people, but not for all. At the same time, we observe that there is a strong feeling in the United States that all those efforts have not made people happier and have not created a 'better world'. The HR community in the United States in our view is still struggling with this and has not come up yet with a credible and effective answer.

Some recent crises in renowned international organizations (Andersen, Enron, WorldCom, Ahold, Parmalat) have further raised the question of how we can build successful and meaningful organizations for the future through engagement. We believe that those organizations that come up with a quick and appropriate answer to this key question will be able to position themselves best and will be able to attract and develop the best human talent. We see a huge challenge for business HR to help businesses to find the right way forward in this context.

The above will require the involvement and engagement of employees at all levels in the organization. Peter Drucker, the famous writer of 33 books, management consultant and university professor who died in 2005, argued convincingly that despite the revolutionary change from manual worker-centred organizations to knowledge worker-based businesses, we are still far from fully using the human capital available to organizations. He believed, in his desire to make everything as simple as possible, that corporations tend to produce too many products and hire employees they don't need. According to him, companies should focus on three things: making a profit, satisfying employees and being socially responsible.

Maximizing the use of human potential will require that we create organizations and jobs that make a meaningful contribution. It will require that we adopt more of an external orientation and combine business success with a worthwhile contribution to the environment and communities we operate in.

We believe that Europe, with its well-established systems and rules for employee participation, is better positioned than the United States to make the move to new, higher levels of employee engagement combined with a greater external component, thereby leading to higher levels of sustainable performance.

The same applies as regards the business HR community in Europe compared to their peers in the United States. For example, the traditional distinction drawn in US companies between unionized and non-unionized units is in our view a thing of the past and will only stand in the way of revitalizing organizations and creating higher levels of employee engagement and business performance. The improved levels of engagement and performance will in our view offer benefits that will outweigh the possible higher costs of an engagement culture.

Another important trend is that, regardless of geography, the new business HR agenda will be determined at international level. Of course selected local businesses will continue to be able to play an important role, but they will eventually have to adopt and follow the business HR standards and agenda set by large companies at international level. Globalization creates new challenges for organizations regarding how to manage their people. The trend within large, decentralized organizations is to centralize the responsibility for determining HR policies and priorities, while decentralizing to management the responsibility for their implementation. Striking the right balance is important to ensure alignment with the business needs at all levels, and effective implementation of HR practices that support the business goals.

The checklist covers the need for a higher degree of engagement of employees at all levels in the organization and better communication and employee feedback through various sections.

Summary

We argued that a proper definition of the new business HR agenda, identifying how the HR function will add value to the organization, must have a higher priority than the reshaping and reorganizing of the function itself (shared service centres).

The checklist can create a breakthrough in many organizations where HR is perceived to lack time to develop strategy.

We believe that in the coming years HR executives must place themselves at the forefront when it comes to new business challenges and the assessment of what the business needs to do regarding the human side of the organization and the building of the capabilities being demanded. HR needs to be able to answer the question 'What business are we in and what are the critical factors for success?'

The checklist can cope with different organizations and their specific features and critical success factors. The checklist leads to the right decisions regarding the areas where HR should put its priorities, efforts and resources. The specifics regarding the HR contribution will vary, but will logically flow from the dialogue around the agreed new business HR agenda.

We believe that the 'bottom-up' use of the checklist is an effective tool with which to define the one- to two-year business HR agenda. The approach is accurate, and defines the business HR agenda in understandable language for all the stakeholders involved.

The differentiating factor for the coming years for the business HR agenda will in our view be to create a higher degree of engagement on the part of employees at all levels in the organization, combined with the concept of organizations doing business successfully but also meaningfully. The latter aspect includes the active external engagement of businesses with the environment and communities they operate in. It will require a greater effort at communication, and employee feedback through the use of surveys. The checklist covers the need for a higher degree of engagement by employees at all levels in the organization, and better communication and employee feedback.

Effective people management requires global HR functions to develop the competencies and skills to agree priority HR practices with line management, practices that are aligned with global HR policies. In the next chapter we will focus on the HR function itself.

4

The new business HR agenda and the HR function

We argue that a proper definition of the new business HR agenda, identifying how the HR function will add value to the organization, must have a higher priority than the reshaping and reorganizing of the function itself (use of technology, shared service centres, outsourcing, etc). This will also be the most effective way to clarify ambiguous expectations regarding the contribution to be delivered by HR.

In many large international companies the shape of the HR function is changing rapidly. In particular, change is driven by the grouping of day-to-day transactional HR processes (payroll, training administration, benefits administration, etc) into shared service centres. The rationale for this is to increase efficiency, drive HR costs down and free up time for the remaining HR professionals in the organization to spend their time on matters that add more value to the business. Ideally, if this can be managed properly, the two activities go together: greater efficiency of the HR function itself is used to create a more concentrated focus on the priority activities that really add value to the organization.

So far, most existing shared service centre organizations for HR have been established at country level (with the United States, given its scale of business, being one of the first), but there is a growing trend to organize such centres regionally, or even globally. IBM is an example of an organization that is successfully managing its transactional HR activities for all operations worldwide through one of its three regional service centres (one in Brazil for the Americas, one in the Philippines for Asia and one in Hungary for Europe, Africa and the Middle East).

In particular, the move to regional shared service centres for HR outside the borders of the home country reshapes the function. The already relatively small local HR teams supporting businesses and other organizations are being further reduced. The skill to negotiate proper service agreements becomes more important. Line managers need to reorientate themselves to the new way of providing HR service, through a distant service centre rather than a local colleague. The remaining, fewer business HR resources need to be clearer than ever before what their contribution to the business will be.

We see the trend to shared service centre organizations as an important one for the coming years. It will require significant investment in technology, process harmonization and systems. It will require significant time and effort from HR leadership to manage the changes and make the new reality come through. But although this activity will be important for the HR function in coming years, it would be a mistake to see it as the main contribution to the business. It is not, in our view. It is largely an internal HR activity. If managed well, it will provide the HR function with the credibility that it is capable of changing its way of working and establishing the most efficient form of organization in a timely fashion.

Our checklist is primarily a tool to help the smaller number of business HR resources that will exist in the future function in such a way as to clarify exactly what their contribution to the business will be. We argue that a proper definition of the new business HR agenda, identifying how the HR function will add value to the organization, must have the highest priority.

Egon Zehnder International undertook a survey in 2004 of 350 directors working in more than 100 cities in North and South America, Europe, the Middle East and Asia. The survey spanned a wide variety of businesses, from small entities to some of the world's largest corporations, and from national to global. In total, the respondents were responsible for the functional leadership of 274,000 HR staff serving 6.5 million employees. The companies they represented had an average turnover of 5 billion euros.

According to the survey, the primary issue remains the tension around the relationship between the HR function and the rest of the business – more specifically, the extent to which HR can help shape business strategy and direction, as opposed to being an order-taker and implementer of plans created by others. At an individual level this sometimes translates into a degree of angst over whether HR directors will ever become a strategic thought partner to the CEO.

The survey concluded that HR directors have too broad a mandate, one that requires different personal capabilities and, ideally, a wide variety of business experience. The six broad areas discussed in the following section indicate what HR directors are actually asked to do today.

Leading business change

Some HR directors not only project-manage the implementation of change efforts but also work with individual executives and groups of managers to lower resistance to change and obtain the necessary buy-in from other levels of the business.

Providing a sounding board

To provide a sounding board, the HR director must have the credibility and stature to become a confidant(e) to the CEO and other executives. Topics range from high-level business strategy development to enhancing board dynamics, helping individuals through personal crises and other sensitive issues.

Acting as the guardian of senior talent management

Senior talent management typically involves the monitoring of the top 50–300 employees.

Managing industrial/employee relations

Leading negotiations and building relations with union and works council partners remains a time-consuming task. In addition, in all companies there is an element of employee relations as well as managing communications and staff feedback.

Managing transactional HR processes

Managing transactional HR processes includes looking after payroll and other administrative activities.

Dealing with other important but non-value-added activities

Monitoring and understanding legal or other regulatory changes, and ensuring compliance, is also part of HR directors' responsibilities. Moreover, there is a growing burden on companies from bodies such as the European Union, which increasingly make time-consuming requests for information.

Clarity of business HR priorities

Egon Zehnder concludes on the basis of the above that it is a hard act for an HR director to lead in the six areas described above with equal capability in all areas. Thus, we believe that there is an urgent case for reviewing the priorities for business HR and for starting with clear and realistic expectations about the shorter-term deliverables for the HR director and the HR function as a whole. This will help to create a realistic, achievable business HR agenda underpinning the business plan and objectives.

If it will not be possible to sort out this dilemma properly and in good time, organizations may decide to outsource some activities and processes. Regional HR service centres for transactional activities could well be the first step in a process that leads to the outsourcing of routine HR activities. Some large companies have already done this (Procter & Gamble, Hewlett Packard, British Petroleum, IBM, etc) or are about to do so. We expect that outsourcing of a number of HR activities will increase in the coming years and also that the number of processes and activities organized through regional HR service centres and outsourcing arrangements will grow. Parts of the recruitment process (from job specification through to the initial selection of applicants against determined criteria) would lend itself to this, as would parts of the learning and training process. The IBM HR Service Centre in Hungary provides not only transactional services but also services that today would normally be considered to be expertise services or business HR responsibilities (for example, the handling of country industrial relations issues for the operations that it serves).

Time is running out. The HR function needs to step up its performance and strengthen its contribution to the business. Clarity on the business HR agenda and the value it will add to the business is of vital importance. Ben Verwaayen, CEO of British Telecom, offers such an approach.

Case study

Ben Verwaayen is sometimes referred to as the most important export product of the Dutch management school. Born in 1952 in the Netherlands, he worked for nine years as President and Managing Director of PTT Telecom, the then state-owned Dutch telecoms company. In 1997 he moved to Lucent Technologies Inc. In 2002 he was appointed to the board of British Telecom and as from 1 February he became the Chief Executive.

Ben made a speech in autumn 2005 for an audience of 350 HR professionals in the Netherlands. The key message he gave was very clear: HR leaders will have to leave their comfort zone and step up their efforts if they want to make a significant business contribution. Instead of accommodating current strategies, HR should play a proactive role when it comes to strategic changes and talent development.

This can be seen as a remarkable statement from the man who is leading a big international company like British Telecom.

Q: What do CEOs such as you do to provide the space to make the HR things you are talking about an integrated part of the overall business strategy?
Ben Verwaayen: Generally speaking, I agree that CEOs do too little. They do not give these topics sufficient thought. They may find it scary to explore new approaches. HR does not challenge them enough in this respect; they leave their bosses too much in the comfort zone.

Q: Which are the most important HR areas?

Ben Verwaayen: The level of education has risen spectacularly over recent decades. Each individual has a contribution to make. Management decisions should reflect this. Our contemporary organizations should provide the space for each individual and team to contribute to the best of its abilities. We are not yet there and there is substantial room for improvement in this area. We often say that the people are our most important asset, but we should live up to this in reality much more than we currently do.

Q: What do you expect from HR?

Ben Verwaayen: HR personnel should come out of their comfort zone. They have an important role to play. When they see opportunities to improve the performance of the business by paying more and better attention to the human side of the business, they should speak up and go for it. This takes courage, but HR needs to do it. I would even expect HR professionals to confront their colleagues in the management team. As a CEO I expect this from HR. HR should not wait for the CEO to take the initiative.

Q: Do you and your colleagues really expect HR to play this confronting role?

Ben Verwaayen: Yes. The question for me is not whether I want this; the issue is how we can get HR leaders to play this role.

Q: How do you manage this yourself?

Ben Verwaayen: I make my expectations with regard to the key contributions from HR pretty explicit. This then also becomes a part of the performance review cycle and an input for reward decisions. I want HR to focus on a few real priorities. And I want HR to stop something like 30 per cent of their existing activities to make room for new things.

Q: Are you happy with the progress so far?

Ben Verwaayen: Generally speaking, I think there is still a long way to go. I will continue to challenge HR about the things that inevitably need to be done on the human side of businesses to improve the overall business performance. HR must come out of their comfort zone and show the courage to confront their colleagues.

We believe the checklist can create a breakthrough in many organizations where the HR director and HR function have too many different sorts of tasks, too many internal clients, a lot of execution and 'therefore' a perceived lack of time for strategy. These organizations need to break out of this vicious circle, and the checklist can help them to do so. The result will be that these organizations will not lose sight of strategic HR considerations on the one hand and will not lose out on available practical action orientation on the other. The checklist combines the two in a seamless manner and creates the common new business HR agenda.

We have referred to the checklist, and how it can be used, on a number of occasions. Before we look at the consistent and successful implementation of people strategy, HR priorities and HR practices, we will first have a look at the checklist itself in Part Two.

The checklist questions

5

The 56 checklist questions

In this part of the book we will focus on the checklist itself. We will do this by giving a brief explanation of each of the 56 questions of the checklist and describing some of the background as to why we are using these specific questions.

We have grouped the 56 questions into nine sections. We will start with an overview of the complete checklist, the nine sections and their relevant questions.

Section 1: Energizing leadership to mobilize people

1. Have there been inspirational events with people from all levels in the organization to create awareness around the vision?
2. Does the leader have a clear vision?
3. Is there clarity in the organization as to what the key priorities in the business are?
4. Have leadership events taken place to accelerate the execution of the strategic priorities?
5. Has it clearly been communicated who is responsible for what?
6. Is there a proper approach in place for a clear delegation of tasks and responsibilities?

Section 2: Build the team

7. Do we have a deep understanding of our members and their strengths and weaknesses?
8. Do we use this understanding to create genuinely balanced teams?
9. Is the legacy that team members have left behind in previous roles in line with the team requirements?
10. Are the ambitions of individuals known and supported by the team?
11. Is the team capable of renewing existing practices?
12. Do the team leadership and climate stimulate diverse opinions and views?

Section 3: Shared vision and values

13. Is there a written statement of what the vision is?
14. Has the vision been elaborated with a larger group of people?
15. Has the vision been communicated to everybody in the business?
16. Are the values aligned with the vision?
17. Are surveys used to check how well the values are being lived?
18. Is the application of variable pay (bonuses) consistent with the vision?

Section 4: Strategic framework

19. Are there just a few clear strategic priorities?
20. Have these been communicated in a compelling and inspiring manner to all key stakeholders?
21. Are strategic priorities translated into concrete and tangible actions?
22. Is it clear what the programme for key innovations will be?
23. Is there overall sufficient level of ambition in the business objectives and plans?
24. Is there a process in place for the rapid reallocation of resources in the event that specific business activities are terminated?

Section 5: Aligned and lean organization

25. Are the targets and work plans aligned with the strategic priorities?
26. Is the organization structure aligned with the strategic priorities?
27. Are organizational processes aligned in such a way as to deliver the strategic priorities?
28. Is the average span of control at least 6?
29. Is the average revenue (output) per manager higher than in comparable organizations?
30. Is the number of management layers smaller than in comparable organizations?

Section 6: High-performing empowered teams

31. Are multifunctional teams in place for the priority activities?
32. Do those teams have clear briefs signed off by the leadership team?
33. Are the teams truly empowered to deliver results?
34. Do those teams have the right tools to perform their tasks?
35. Is there formal training to accelerate teamwork?
36. Is there a process for systematic review of required team skills and competencies?
37. Is the leadership competency model being used to drive winning behaviour?

Section 7: Coaching: develop yourself and others to win

38. Is there a clear definition of 'talent development', a definition that is understood by most people?
39. Is it clear what support line managers can give to help improve individual performance?
40. Are individual targets clear and seen as stretching but achievable?
41. Is it well articulated how 'coaching' can contribute to a better leadership style?
42. Has this organization a stimulating coaching culture?
43. Have board members and other key people received training in coaching?

Section 8: Create a winning organizational climate

44. Is the leadership style genuinely seen as positive?
45. Are surveys being used to measure progress regarding the organizational climate?
46. Are successes being celebrated?
47. Do people generally feel recognized for what they do?
48. Are regrettable losses of people avoided?
49. Can the organization attract the right people?
50. Is the organization a good place to work in?
51. Are the targets and the target-setting process generating positive energy?

Section 9: Deliver results and reward

52. Have business results been delivered against targets in at least two out of the past three years?
53. Has variable pay (bonuses) at least been at 'par' level on average over the past three years?
54. Are results regularly shared with a wider group of people?
55. Are people rewarded in other ways, apart from by cash payments?
56. Is time in job sufficient to enable a 'delivery culture'?

We will now give a brief explanation of each of the 56 questions of the checklist and describe some of the background as to why we are using these specific questions. It is important to understand what it is we want to clarify through each of the questions.

1. Have there been inspirational events with people from all levels in the organization to create awareness around the vision?

Many of today's organizations are smart enough to organize events around the vision of the company. There are two important elements being checked through this question. The first is that it is not good enough to arrange such events with a selected group of just a few people. This denies the power of large numbers of operators at all levels in the organization. Think about the comments of Peter Drucker about knowledge workers, to which we have already referred in this book. The second additional element lies in the word 'inspirational'. There is no single recipe for what inspirational events should look like, but we have given a couple of aspects that can be looked at. The essence is that people need to be approached in a holistic way and not just by throwing words at them through PowerPoint presentations. People need to be inspired and mobilized through their mind and through their heart. There are many ways to do this, and we will show a few practical examples in the next part of the book.

2. Does the leader have a clear vision?

The answer to this question is not so obvious as it seems. Many of us will find it impossible to see how a leader without a clear vision can survive. We need to be aware, though, that it can sometimes take a relatively long period of time for the leader to crystallize the vision for his or her organization. Can you imagine the thinking process the respective CEOs of companies like Nokia and Mannesmann must have gone through? They had to become clear in their mind first that their companies had to be transformed from (machine) manufacturing and technical companies into fast-moving mobile phone and telecommunications companies like Nokia and Vodafone (Mannesmann became part of the global Vodafone company).

If the vision is not clear, this causes some major problems for some of the topics to follow. In such situations, however, the key question is what the top team is doing to come to a clear vision. The worst of all worlds is for the vision not to be clear, but also not being worked on and elaborated by the leadership team.

PART TWO

3. Is there clarity in the organization as to what the key priorities in the business are?

We are assuming that there is some sort of hierarchy between vision and key priorities. First comes the vision and then the key priorities. We are aware that things do not always work in this way in reality. The reality is much more fluid and sometimes much more confusing. But, to go back to the example of Nokia and Mannesmann, just imagine that a new or changed vision is not followed by deliberate decisions about what the key priorities in the business are. We have seen quite a number of companies, though, that have left their key priorities more or less intact, while the long-term direction was changing.

4. Have leadership events taken place to accelerate the execution of the strategic priorities?

We describe some examples in our book of how leadership events can help to accelerate the execution of strategic priorities. The key elements we are checking here are speed and energy. The execution of strategic priorities cannot be forced and rushed. It normally takes hard work over a long period to make things happen. But the initial process of execution at leadership level can surely be accelerated by having a series of well-thought-through leadership events. Our experience is that this generates lots of positive energy.

5. Has it clearly been communicated who is responsible for what?

Although this seems a rather harmless question, we have learned from the use of the checklist that this question in the leadership section is answered significantly less positively than the other questions in the same section.

The key factor is that leadership teams need not only to provide clarity about the vision, strategic priorities, etc, but also to come to an agreement among themselves about who will be responsible for what in the light of the vision and the strategic priorities. Once that is done, the key issue seems to be the clarification of this to the wider organization. If it is not done properly, especially in large, complex organizations, room is given to all sorts of well-meant initiatives, in various parts of the organization, that may not be fully consistent. We are not making a plea here for a Stalinist approach, but discipline can be important. Discipline is achieved by being clear up front how things are organized and who is responsible for what.

6. Is there a proper approach in place for a clear delegation of tasks and responsibilities?

This question is primarily about the operating framework. Large organizations need to be explicit about how they are organized. Delegation is just one element of such a framework, but an important one. If there is no clarity on this, the chances are that duplication of work or gaps in terms of responsibilities will occur, and this is not good. We have chosen to check delegation specifically, since we see a worrying trend in some companies whereby unclear systems of delegation lead to confusion in the execution, and eventually to suboptimal performance. The response of top leadership in a number of cases has been to say, 'If they cannot get things done as we want them to be done, we will do it ourselves'. This centralized approach may initially feel good, but creates much frustration. In these situations it is advisable to review the operating framework if necessary and further clarify the system of delegation that the company wants to maintain.

7. Do we have a deep understanding of our members and their strengths and weaknesses?

This question is answered positively less often than we had expected. What looks like a basic requirement in modern organizations is not always there. We believe that two elements play a role here. The first is that in large international organizations people move from one job to another frequently, and sometimes from one country to another. Not all companies collect and keep the relevant data about a person in a systematic way. Second, we normally collect some data about the performance of a person, but we generally do this on the basis of the dominant system. For example, if we assess people on the basis of an existing competency model, we may fail to keep track of how the person has delivered against the work plan and targets throughout the years. We may also miss out on some other aspects of performance and the person. If new team members are appointed from outside the company, this issue may be even more significant.

8. Do we use this understanding to create genuinely balanced teams?

One's natural inclination is to look primarily at individual qualities and then at the team. We are not arguing that one should reverse the order, but it can be quite revealing to take an existing team and create an overall picture of the available skills, competencies, experience, etc. In almost all cases, gaps and overlaps will show. It is important to be aware of this and to remedy the gaps as quickly as possible. Overlapping skills and competencies are less of an issue, but can lead to a preferred way of working in the team that is not always optimal for the challenges that need to be mastered. If four out of five team members are strong in creating a vision and breakthrough thinking, but relatively weak in building commitment for the vision with others, and in team leadership, there may be an issue in turning the vision into reality.

9. Is the legacy that team members have left behind in previous roles in line with the team requirements?

This question has a link with question 7. The focus for this question is whether an organization makes use of knowledge about a person's track record when a decision needs to be made about a new team member. We define legacy and track record in a broader sense: What experience does a person have? What skills and competencies were displayed successfully and consistently in different jobs? What were his or her remarkable successes? What is the person really known for? And so on.

The other aspect measured through this question is whether the team requirements have been looked at systematically and whether an assessment has been made as to how a (new) team member would best fit with the team.

10. Are the ambitions of individuals known and supported by the team?

When a new team member is recruited, normally the ambitions a candidate has are covered through the interviewing and selection process. An existing team and team members have their ambitions as well. Their ambitions may evolve or fundamentally change over time, for example as result of a change in their personal situation. A good team finds ways to address this and creates an open climate where ambitions can be discussed and where others are supported to realize their ambitions. This should not be dependent on formal systems, meetings, etc, but be a natural element of the team conversations. Team members should invest in each other's development.

11. Is the team capable of renewing existing practices?

A team can perform well, but lack the ability to renew and innovate. If this gap exists in a team, one should first examine whether some members of the team could play their role in a different way, paying less attention to maintaining the existing situation and instead focusing on renewal activities. If this is not possible, it is important to change the team so as to add this capability.

12. Do the team leadership and climate stimulate diverse opinions and views?

We will address the importance of diversity for good teamwork later on. Well-managed diversity creates the opportunity for a team to excel in performance. It does need to be well managed, though, and this is where the role of the leader is vital. If it is not managed well, it is likely that the performance of the team will become mediocre, and not as good as could be expected on the basis of its members' individual capabilities. We know that individual team members in excellent teams are sometimes encouraged by the leader to represent a different view from the others. The objective of this is simply to get all the cards on the table before a decision is reached. In such teams it will not be an issue when an individual member of the team has a view that diverges from that of the majority of the team even when that view is not stimulated by the leader. The climate in such a team will allow that person to come up with a minority view, and the leader will address how to handle this, after a decision has been made. A team with such a climate is fundamentally better than a team without it. Daily examples of the consequences of a bad team climate can be observed in every organization, on television, in newspapers, in politics, etc.

13. Is there a written statement of what the vision is?

This question is not meant to check whether someone in a large organization has a written vision statement somewhere in a drawer. We are checking whether sufficient effort has been given to carefully writing a statement on the vision, as a necessary step to enable broader communication of the vision.

14. Has the vision been elaborated with a larger group of people?

Sometimes it can be lonely at the top when a new vision is being worked on. However, sooner or later more people will have to be engaged. When we talk about a 'larger group of people' in this context, we are not thinking in terms of hundreds or thousands of people. The starting point for engaging this larger group normally is a vision, with some fixed key elements, built around some new insights, but still lots of things to be studied, discussed and decided. Involving the larger group in a timely fashion can be very exciting for the people involved and create high levels of commitment for the execution that will follow later. The engagement process needs to be well organized and orchestrated. It needs to be clear what the non-negotiables are. A situation where discussions continue for too long a period should be avoided and it should be clear what the rules for decision making are.

15. Has the vision been communicated to everybody in the business?

The logical next step is to communicate the vision to the wider organization. Every communication will immediately say that this needs to be done in a professional manner, not using abstract business language for all levels in the organization, but tailoring the form and shape of the communication to various audiences in the organization. If done properly, this can create a strong sense of direction and commitment, and it can create momentum and excitement.

PART TWO

16. Are the values aligned with the vision?

We could also ask the question the other way round: is the vision aligned with the values? In some companies where the values are very strong and play a very tangible role (eg IKEA), it may be more appropriate to start with the values. The point we are making here is that the values and vision must never contradict each other.

If one of the values of a company is sustainability (in its relationships with suppliers, customers and consumers, in its products, in its employee relations, etc), that company cannot embrace a vision that foresees innovations, products, ways of doing business, etc that oppose the principle of sustainability. In reality, things are sometimes not as black and white as described in the previous sentence, and therefore are more difficult to assess. Our experience is that those who work in or with a specific company have more than sufficient information to answer the question promptly.

17. Are surveys used to check how well the values are being lived?

Values, values statements and values programmes are useless if they do not drive behaviours. The behaviours that can be observed in a company are the visible expression of values. In cases where the behaviours and the values are not aligned, there is the risk that the company will move in the wrong direction. Surveys are an effective instrument to measure the degree of alignment.

18. Is the application of variable pay (bonuses) consistent with the vision?

The issue of variable pay seems to have been around for too long now. There are still many situations where variable pay at its best has become a hygiene factor, but certainly does not function as a stimulus to go the extra mile – which is what it should do. A higher than expected number of checklist respondents have answered this question negatively. Therefore, it may be helpful to go back to the basics. Ask yourself what in essence your vision sets out to do and then take this as a starting point for the variable pay system. If your vision is about growth and your variable pay system is based on profit, you know you have a problem. What helps, in our view, is to manage the application of the variable pay in a way that is not too far away from the operation concerned. Large organizations sometimes try to have one system for the totality of complex international businesses. That is mission impossible. Going back to basics, back to the essence of what you are trying to do, and using this as the starting point for your variable pay system, is important. Combining this approach with some freedom in managing the application of the system as close as possible to the relevant unit is in our view the most effective way to create consistency between the application of variable pay and the vision.

19. Are there just a few clear strategic priorities?

The key word in this question is 'few'. It is understandable that at the top of large organizations more than three strategic priorities may exist. Some of these strategic priorities will reflect the specific mission that some of the business units need to accomplish. The number of corporate priorities relevant to all parts of the business, however, needs to be very limited. Lists of strategic priorities for business units with more than 10 topics or so are 'suspicious'. Any points mentioned from position 11 onwards are in any case neither strategic nor priorities. There is evidence that having five strategic priorities is already on the high side.

20. Have these been communicated in a compelling and inspiring manner to all key stakeholders?

This question assumes that management has been able to identify the few strategic priorities that really matter. Normally a lot of attention is given to communicating what those priorities are. This question aims to check whether the way in which the communication of priorities is done is 'compelling' and 'inspiring'. 'Compelling' means that the message is delivered not once, but multiple times so that nobody can miss it. 'Inspiring' means that the message sticks. The communication is done in understandable ways that everybody can relate to. Both mind and heart are being touched.

21. Are strategic priorities translated into concrete and tangible actions?

Once the few strategic priorities have been clarified and communicated, the next step needs to be made. Normally, strategic priorities are formulated in pretty broad terms. There are various expressions used for what we here call strategic priorities: key strategic thrusts, must-win battles, etc. They are a good starting point for establishing more concrete plans of action. This requires much work, but is a useful way to give meaning to the broader strategic priorities.

22. Is it clear what the programme for key innovations will be?

For any organization it is a must to innovate. This is an ongoing activity and requires ongoing communication about the key innovations. For the people side of the business, knowledge about the innovation programme is important. It allows talent to go and explore new job opportunities that are important to the overall business. It also allows the formation of teams of talented people, in many cases cross-border teams.

PART TWO

23. Is there overall sufficient level of ambition in the business objectives and plans?

The answer to this question is not so easy to give. In different stages of development of a business the ambition level may differ. We are trying to measure here whether, given the stage a business finds itself in, sufficient effort is made to benchmark the company against competitors and to find ways forward. For public companies the financial markets and financial analysts may play an important role in keeping the company alert. We would argue that customer satisfaction or dissatisfaction may be an even better measure for keeping the company on its toes.

24. Is there a process in place for the rapid reallocation of resources in the event that specific business activities are terminated?

In a company that renews itself, that has a clear vision and strategic priorities, that has a good innovation programme and that has the ambition to be in the top league, clear choices will have to be made from time to time. Putting the money and resources where the mouth is, is crucial. As a consequence, other activities will have to be stopped. In many organizations we observe that this process is not well organized. This can lead to situations where all the old activities are being continued, while the new priorities are being added to an increasing list of things that must be done. As long as sufficient resources exist, the 'old' will most likely continue to receive lots of attention. Therefore, it is important that the modern organization develop the capability to swiftly shift resources from less important activities to the most important ones. This does not necessarily mean restructuring. Many people who worked on 'old' activities need to be prepared to go and apply their skills and competencies on other projects. Training may be needed to enhance new skills and competencies.

25. Are the targets and work plans aligned with the strategic priorities?

This question is to some extent related to question 21, although the present question is more focused on actions and plans at organizational level. Most of what is said in relation to question 21 also applies in the case of this question. In addition, this question measures the extent to which individual targets and work plans are aligned with the strategic priorities.

PART TWO

26. Is the organization structure aligned with the strategic priorities?

In the case of strategic change, one of the important dimensions to be reviewed and aligned is the organizational structure. This needs to be done in a timely and pragmatic fashion. The reality in many large organizations today is that it is not possible to apply one set of simplistic organization design principles throughout the totality of the organization. Some business units may have to be structured in a different manner as compared with others within the same company. In large international organizations, matrix set-ups are almost unavoidable. Whatever the solution may be, the organizational structure needs to reflect the strategic priorities in the business. If Nestlé sees its Nespresso business as a global business and as an area where high growth can be achieved by applying one brand and one approach worldwide, Nespresso will have to be managed by a team that holds global profit and loss responsibility for Nespresso. The performance of Nespresso would be damaged if Nespresso activities in different countries were to be made dependent on the priority that a specific country gives to Nespresso, depending on the overall portfolio of Nestlé activities in that country and the relative importance of Nespresso in that country compared to other Nestlé product categories. Therefore, we say 'horses for courses': avoid dogmatic approaches and see to it that organizational structure follows strategy. Any obstacles to delivering the strategy success-fully should be swiftly removed.

27. Are organizational processes aligned in such a way as to deliver the strategic priorities?

The Nespresso example can also be used to clarify this question. Managing the Nespresso brand is clearly a global matter. The same could apply for sourcing and supply, whereas the customer development activities most likely require strong sales forces on the ground, locally, working closely together with customers. Again, 'horses for courses': avoid dogmas and ensure that the processes follow the strategy. Any obstacles to delivering the strategy successfully should be swiftly removed.

28. Is the average span of control at least 6?

We define span of control as the number of people that a single line manager has reporting to him or her. The average span of control can be found by carrying out this calculation for all line managers in the organization. Research clearly shows that poorly performing organizations tend to have a low average span of control, say 3 or 4, or even lower. The same research shows that higher-performing companies have a much higher span of control, going up to as much as an average of 20 direct reports per line manager. We have chosen an average span of control of 6 as the minimum. This question measures the effectiveness of the organization. The span of control is also important for the number of managers in an organization. If a company had 1,000 operators in total and an average span of control of 5, then 200 line managers would be needed. To manage those 200, 40 middle managers would be needed and they would report to some eight senior managers. In total, there would thus be three management layers. If the same company had an average span of control of 10, then 100 managers would be needed, and 10 senior managers to manage those 100 – in total, two management layers.

29. Is the average revenue (output) per manager higher than in comparable organizations?

This question is a check for productivity. The revenue per manager can vary enormously in different sorts of businesses and therefore comparisons between organizations in different sectors and industries are not useful. On the other hand, comparisons between companies in a single sector or industry can be very helpful and revealing. Even simpler is the comparison between comparable units within one and the same company.

30. Is the number of management layers smaller than in comparable organizations?

Building on what we said under question 28, we can further check the organization's effectiveness by comparing the number of management layers with that in comparable organizations. We find this important, since the existence of too many management layers not only is costly but also carries the risk of over-managing and suffocating the organization. Decision making tends to be slower and more cumbersome in organizations with too many management layers.

31. Are multifunctional teams in place for the priority activities?

Teams are a flexible way to organize work and activities that are urgent and important. Strategic challenges normally require the input from various disciplines. In large international organizations, multifunctional teams are a must. Organizations that are too strongly focused on functional silos will therefore find it more difficult to form teams that can deal effectively with priority tasks.

32. Do those teams have clear briefs signed off by the leadership team?

Teams need to have a clear and challenging direction set by the leadership team. Clarity is needed to provide orientation to the team and its members. Challenge is required to motivate the team. The combination of the two leads to engaged teams. We believe that a formal process for signing off briefs for new teams and projects and for deciding to stop other activities needs to feature on the leadership agenda. It is amazing to observe how many 'informal' teams and projects exist at any point in time in virtually every large organization.

PART TWO

33. Are the teams truly empowered to deliver results?

Teams need to have the authority to manage their own work and the internal processes within the team. The team needs to be composed of members who have relevant skills and competencies. The team should be the right size, and the mix of members needs to be appropriate. The wider organization needs to support the work to be done by the team and needs to recognize the importance of the work.

34. Do those teams have the right tools to perform their tasks?

Training and technical assistance need to be available to support the work of the team. Information and information systems need to be available, and if this is not the case, the team should have the authority to organize proper support in this area and support for other material resources.

35. Is there formal training to accelerate teamwork?

In many cases, teams do not take the time to be trained at the start of the work. It is often felt that there is no time for training in that phase of the work. This is questionable. More than in other stages of the work to be done, training is effective at the start, especially if the objective of that training is to kick-start the team. For example, in a research and development organization it was decided to start each new project with project management skills training for the project team. An integral part of the training was to clarify the brief and work it out in a detailed project plan. Another real task that was accomplished as part of the training was a plan for managing the key stakeholders. The fact that each new team went through the same training meant that the teams developed similar skills and a common approach to project management. The project management capabilities were really elevated to a higher level than ever before.

36. Is there a process for systematic review of required team skills and competencies?

Depending on the task of the team (get work done, or coordinate activities, or provide support to other teams, etc), it will need to be decided what skills and competencies are required for successful completion of the task. Often this is done in a haphazard way. A more rigorous approach to exploring and determining the critical skills and competencies can avoid the team being confronted with gaps in skills and competencies at a later stage of the work.

37. Is the leadership competency model being used to drive winning behaviour?

Further to question 36, the availability of a competency model helps greatly to define the required skills and competencies. The same model provides guidance regarding behaviours that are seen as positive. The competency model normally also is explicit about the way that teams are expected to work together and the role of individuals as part of teams. And the model clarifies what is expected from team leaders. Altogether, this gives an important indication of what are seen as 'winning behaviours'.

38. Is there a clear definition of 'talent development', a definition that is understood by most people?

One could say that every organization has some sort of 'talent development' approach. For example, even a small organization with, say, 10 employees will go a long way to keep the new recruit who turns out to be a very talented colleague, someone certainly capable of being promoted in the future to a job with a higher level of responsibility. If the organization is not able to offer such a job in the future, the person may not stay. A worse situation occurs if the company is not even willing to consider options that could make it eventually possible for a job with a higher level of responsibility to be offered to that person. In this case we would describe the 'talent development' approach of the company as poor. In the latter case it is likely that the 10 colleagues of the person who leaves would understand his or her reasons for leaving the company. The point is that what we call 'talent development' is real and tangible in any organization. In bigger organizations, at some point the need will arise to be more explicit about 'talent development'. A bigger organization also has to be able to explain to potential recruits what good people can expect regarding the opportunities they will encounter for developing their talent.

This question about a clear definition of 'talent development', one that is understood by most people, is not aiming at having one 'textbook' definition across different organizations. Every organization must find its own way to clarify what is meant by 'talent development'. It is worth investing some time and effort in this, regardless of the size of the organization.

39. Is it clear what support line managers can give to help improve individual performance?

The line manager is a key factor in making the relationship between an individual and an organization work. The Career Innovation Group has pointed out that the conversations between leaders and members of their team are an important vehicle. Many topics are expected to be dealt with in those conversations. To mention some: clarity about what is expected in terms of work today, feedback on how they are performing, development for the future, reward, skill development for the current job, work–life balance and workload, etc. The Career Innovation Group found that there are ample opportunities to improve those conversations. The more honest, personal, constructive and future oriented those conversations are, the better they will work. Getting it right will build trust between the leader and the incumbent, and will motivate and inspire performance.

40. Are individual targets clear and seen as stretching but achievable?

Question 25 deals with the alignment of targets with the strategic priorities. Here we are checking whether the targets themselves are seen as fair. The assessment as to whether they are or not will always be subjective. Putting down targets in writing is useful and to be recommended, but it does not guarantee that those targets are seen as stretching but achievable. Our experience is that it is hard work and time-consuming to get it right. We argue that at least a few solid discussions are necessary to properly clarify the targets and agree them with the incumbent. However, it is time well spent. Clarity concerning what is expected from an individual, and the support that the individual expects, lies at the basis of any successful working relationship.

41. Is it well articulated how 'coaching' can contribute to a better leadership style?

It is important for an organization to have a clear view of how coaching can improve the leadership style. There are some key elements that need to be looked at. First there is the dimension of developing the individual coaching competencies. This is important for the individual, but will also help line managers to improve their coaching of other people. Second, if coaching capabilities are developed and improved for a broader group of people in the organization, this will have an impact on the organizational climate overall. Coaching capabilities become a key building block of leadership. Third, there is the issue of a coaching culture.

42. Has this organization a stimulating coaching culture?

Following question 41 and building on what is said there, it is clear that building a coaching culture requires significant investment and time. If done properly, this will surely lead to a stimulating coaching culture. In such a culture people find it important to give attention to helping others to do things better. Doing things better is good for the individual and for the organization overall. It builds trust and stimulates teamwork.

PART TWO

43. Have board members and other key people received training in coaching?

We want to check here whether the top leadership is committed to coaching. If, as described under questions 41 and 42, companies want to invest in developing individual coaching competencies, in coaching capabilities as a key element of leadership and in building a coaching culture, the top team must actively take part in this process. The leaders must live the behaviours they want to see in others. The commitment to participate in training events is a powerful way to show this commitment.

44. Is the leadership style genuinely seen as positive?

The phrase 'the smell of the place' is sometimes used to describe the sensation that one gets when going to a company and stepping into the reception area. Immediately one starts to build up a perception about many things in the company that one is not aware of at that point in time. The size of the reception area, the colours, the way one is greeted by the person at the reception desk, etc are all pieces of information that contribute to 'the smell of the place'.

It is no different with leadership style. A few first impressions are often sufficient to create 'the leadership smell of the place'. It is clearly not good enough to base an assessment of the leadership style on first impressions alone, but the fact that first impressions do give a hint of the leadership style shows that there normally is a collective awareness and appreciation of that style.

45. Are surveys being used to measure progress regarding the organizational climate?

Surveys are an obvious tool with which to measure the climate in an organization more accurately. Many companies have decided to organize surveys regularly. It is through a series of surveys that progress can be measured properly. The organizational climate is one of the issues to be looked at, and normally this will be done through a set of individual items in the survey. Although we have seen many positive answers to this question in the checklist, there are still a considerable number of companies not using surveys in a systematic manner.

46. Are successes being celebrated?

In some cultures it is normal to celebrate successes. In most cultures, though, celebration of success does not happen naturally and needs to be organized. Everybody who has been part of a successful company, project or team knows how motivating it is to share the feeling of success with colleagues.

We are not checking, through this question, whether the culture of an organization foresees, in a constructive and positive way, how it will handle failures. However, the handling of failures can be as important as the celebration of success.

PART TWO

47. Do people generally feel recognized for what they do?

What has been said under question 44 about 'the smell of the place' can also be used to explain what we want to check here. The question seeks an answer concerning the general perception in an organization regarding the recognition of people and what they do. Any organization that has difficulty in answering this question positively has an issue. Many things may be in place (good job, clear responsibilities, competitive reward package, etc), but if the recognition is not there, or at least is not felt, it will be impossible to create deeper levels of commitment (commitment with the mind and the heart).

48. Are regrettable losses of people avoided?

Answering this question accurately assumes that a process or system is in place to measure the number of losses of people overall and the number of regretted losses more specifically. In Unilever's ice cream organization a report was prepared every month which listed the names of the individual managers who had left the business. It was indicated on the basis of information available from other HR processes which of the people on the list had shown sustained high performance and which of them were considered as having high potential. These cases were investigated specifically. This sounds, and is, straightforward. It is important to note, however, that the monthly report contained information about departing managers for all ice cream operations in 40 countries.

49. Can the organization attract the right people?

In the late 1990s much discussion took place about the 'War for Talent'. Under the influence of the New Economy it was questioned whether traditional companies would be able to maintain their attractiveness for talented people. Despite the fact that the New Economy had a major setback and was not able to sustain its initial success, the question whether traditional companies are still attractive enough remains. The 'War for Talent' is far from over. Rather than compete with New Economy companies, young, talented people today are not taking it for granted that the well-known large international companies are the most attractive environment to work in. Many turn away from those companies and go and work for governments, the United Nations, the European Union or similar international institutions, or start their own business.

This question is an important one and requires careful consideration. When companies run into visible difficulties in attracting the right people (for example, hardly any university graduates showing up for a company presentation at a recruitment fair), a lot of other things have started to go wrong long before that. The problems may have to do with poor financial results, ongoing restructuring, scandals or with a whole range of HR practices that can have an influence on the perception of the company.

50. Is the organization a good place to work in?

Let us assume that an organization is attractive enough to attract the right people. Once those talented people have joined, the question is whether they commit themselves to the organization, to their day-to-day work, to their line manager and to the team they are part of. If they do, this will have two very important benefits. First, they will enjoy the work and probably be willing to go beyond the call of duty. Second, they will intend to stay with the organization. This commitment is likely to grow in organizations that are good places to work in. If the organization is not a good place to work in and the commitment does not exist, two effects can be observed. First, people will not be willing to go the extra mile and will just do what is asked of them. Second, people will seriously consider leaving the organization once an opportunity occurs.

51. Are the targets and the target-setting process generating positive energy?

Targets and target setting are a recurring theme. First, the vision and strategy of an organization become tangible through the work plan and the targets of an individual. Second, as part of day-to-day coaching the question needs to be asked how individuals can improve their performance, assuming that the targets are stretching but achievable. And third, the targets pop up again when the achievement against the targets needs to be assessed as a basis for determining variable pay. Targets play an important role throughout the year and therefore it is vital to get them right. Whereas 'impossible' targets will lead to negative energy, realistic targets can become a source of positive energy.

52. Have business results been delivered against targets in at least two out of the past three years?

This is a simple question that cannot always be answered positively. We assume that business results are normally one of the key measures affecting variable pay. We also assume that the setting of targets is done in a fair manner. If, in this context, the business results are not achieved two out of three times, there is a serious issue. There can be many reasons why the targets have been missed, although generic economic circumstances certainly should not be blamed. Primarily, the reasons for not making the targets should be sought within the organization itself.

53. Has variable pay (bonuses) at least been at 'par' level on average over the past three years?

The previous question was intended to check the degree of success at organizational level, whereas this question focuses more on the individual level. We shall first explain what is meant by 'par'. In every variable pay or bonus system there is a 'par' level. This represents the payout or bonus that will be given if the targets have been met. The achievement has been good, the targets have been delivered, no more and no less than that. This approach makes it allowable to give a higher bonus to those who have 'over-delivered' or to give a lower than 'par' bonus to those who have 'under-delivered'. For example, for a specific group of people the 'par' bonus is, say, 10 per cent, with a minimum of zero and a maximum of 20 per cent. Our expectation is that in any organization, variable pay over a period of three years ought to have been at least at 'par' level, ie 10 per cent in this example. In any one year the average may have been lower or higher, but we expect an average of at least 10 per cent.

Unlike in question 52, we are not solely looking at the business results dimension of the variable pay. For a proper answer to question 53 we need to be aware that personal targets and possibly other elements are also included when we speak about variable pay.

54. Are results regularly shared with a wider group of people?

Feedback is important so that work on the improvement of the performance can start. Feedback can be provided in many different ways, but we believe that one-to-one feedback is the most effective. E-mail letters from a leader to a large group of people are far less effective, but e-mail does offer an opportunity to give information – the same information to a larger number of people. A way of working that is intermediate between one-to-one feedback, on the one hand, and communication to a large group, on the other, involves regular meetings where people can attend and where the leader is present to give an update on performance and results. Financial results will surely feature in this sort of meeting, but other themes or issues can be addressed too. Such a meeting also offers an opportunity for the audience to ask questions.

PART TWO

55. Are people rewarded in other ways, apart from by cash payments?

Question 47 has already referred to the importance of recognition for creating commitment. It is important for employees to receive a good bonus if they have delivered an excellent performance, but it may be equally important for them to be recognized for other activities that have gone well, especially activities carried out publicly for a wider audience. There are numerous things happening in an organization that can be used to express gratitude for what has been done. It may be as simple as mentioning in a large meeting that one of the employees has done a good job. Or an article in the company magazine about the logistics department that has managed to raise service levels significantly. Or an annual award given to the team voted by other teams as having lived the values of the company in a remarkably positive manner.

56. Is time in job sufficient to enable a 'delivery culture'?

Time in job is one of the red threads running through this book. Research shows that successful companies tend to have leaders who stay longer with the organization. Jim Collins has said powerful things about this in his book *Good to Great*. Many large organizations are struggling with this, and have managers frequently moving from one job to another internally. In a major fast-moving consumer goods company in Europe the average time in job in the marketing function is below two years. This can mean that a marketing manager comes to a job, analyses market research data, proposes one or two changes to the product portfolio, prepares these changes up to launch and then moves on to the next job. A new marketing manager comes into the job and manages the launch of the changes. Some things work, others don't; the new marketing manager wants some alterations. And so it goes. This sounds ridiculous, but is reality. In an organization with such low time in job, it will not be possible to establish a 'delivery culture'. People leave the job before they have been able to see the effect of the things they have set in motion.

On the other hand, we do not advise leaving people in their jobs as long as possible. The right balance needs to be struck. This is not easy and the balance may be different in different sectors.

PART TWO

Understanding the checklist to enable dialogue and implementation

6

Section 1: Energizing leadership to mobilize people

In this part of the book we will go through each of the nine sections of the checklist. In Part Two we gave a brief explanation of each of the 56 questions, which underpin the nine sections. In the coming nine chapters we will give further background information regarding each of the sections as a whole. We will use short practical case studies and short summaries of pieces of research to illustrate the points that we find important.

Energizing leadership to mobilize people

- Have there been inspirational events with people from all levels in the organization to create awareness around the vision?
- Does the leader have a clear vision?
- Is there clarity in the organization as to what the key priorities in the business are?
- Have leadership events taken place to accelerate the execution of the strategic priorities?
- Has it been clearly communicated who is responsible for what?
- Is there a proper approach in place for clear delegation of tasks and responsibilities?

Introduction

Leadership is one of those words that is used so often and with so many different meanings that it has almost become a 'commodity'. Despite that, there is consensus that leadership is vital for any organization. It is hard to think of a high-performing organization with a business HR agenda without 'Leadership' and 'Leadership Development' featuring on it.

We use the phrase 'Energizing leadership to mobilize people' as the title of this chapter. It encapsulates our belief that leaders should put more of their energy into mobilizing the people they work with. Doing so does not replace existing leadership tasks. On top of existing leadership competencies, we see the building of deeper levels of engagement and commitment than we have experienced so far as a new leadership task and competency. It is a key challenge for the future.

Before we explain this further, we want to clarify what 'Energizing leadership to mobilize people' is not about.

Energizing leadership: what it is not

First, energizing leadership is not a new leadership style. Different leadership styles can be identified – democratic, pacesetting, coaching, authoritative, coercive, etc – each having a different impact on the organizational climate. Also, it is accepted that leaders need to have the capability to use different leadership styles depending on the situation and the concrete work that needs to be done.

The case is no different for energizing leadership. Energizing leaders use different leadership styles effectively as well. Some styles will work well with energizing leaders, others less so. For example, a coercive leadership style surely is not very effective for building deeper levels of engagement in any organization. On the other hand, an authoritarian leadership style may work well for energizing leaders in some organizations, whereas in other organizations it would not. The point is that energizing leaders use different leadership styles, like any other leader.

Second, energizing leadership to mobilize people is not just about the leadership as displayed by the CEO and very few leaders around the CEO. Energizing leadership is about the leadership displayed at various levels in the organization. 'Leadership starts at the top' is an often-used phrase. We believe this statement to be true, but we need to realize that it is not true for the top leadership alone. Leadership starts at the top, but must always be followed by a structured approach to establish proper leadership at various levels in the organization.

Case study: Making great leaders

A Fortune 30 heavy manufacturing company with revenues of approximately $30 billion needed to meet its demand for leaders around the globe. This company had experienced explosive growth, both domestically and in emerging markets such as China and India. The company understood that there had to be a more integrated approach to leadership development, an approach that could ensure the growth of leadership skills in a manner that allowed for accountability and consistency around the globe.

Three leadership competency models were developed, focusing on executives, managers and supervisors respectively. Each model had a core set of behavioural expectations with differences based on level and impact on the company. Each of the competency models was clustered into three categories: Vision (with an emphasis on strategic development); Execute (focused on getting it done now); and Legacy (developing capabilities for the future). The competency models were then used to develop a fully tailored leadership development programme (entitled 'Making Great Leaders').

The programme was implemented across the United States, Europe (including the United Kingdom), Australia, Singapore, Russia and China. The implementation strategy was to put the senior executives through the programme quickly, then cascade the effort to lower levels. The speed was a critical variable, as this was the only way to impact a company of 85,000 people. The result has been that the CEO, all group presidents, most vice-presidents and department heads have attended. They have all created development plans that have been reviewed by their superiors and are now in the process of implementation. Managers and supervisors around the company are now attending the programme.

> The result of the programme has been the creation of a new
> language within the company. For the first time, people speak of the
> style of leadership they are using, the climate they are creating and how
> they need to intervene to develop the leaders below them.

It is difficult to see how large international organizations could act other-
wise. We observe it as a trend, though, that even in large international
organizations the call for clear leadership to be shown by the very top
leaders can be heard regularly. We believe that this should be understood
as a signal that leadership at different levels and in different geographical
locations should be better aligned than may be the case in the reality of
large international organizations today. It should not be interpreted as an
invitation for 'do as you are told' leadership.

The emergence of so-called celebrity CEOs in a number of organizations
is not necessarily the right response to a call for better leadership. If such
a new leader is recruited because of the reputation that person has gained
in a previous role, it could easily go wrong. We would advocate that in
any case the requirements for any leadership role are always analysed
thoroughly before recruiting and appointing a person. This applies to CEO
roles as well, and the chance that a 'celebrity CEO' who gained a good
reputation somewhere else will also fit into your organization is relatively
low. Also, putting a 'celebrity CEO' in a new environment with a different
set of requirements in terms of competencies and skills may be a real
stretch for some of the big egos behind 'celebrity CEOs'.

In fact, executive search firms confirm that the 'macho' concept behind
the 'celebrity CEOs' does not work. Rather, team players with a healthy
portion of emotional intelligence are sought.

Third, energizing leadership to mobilize people is not primarily about
culture. No doubt energizing leaders who mobilize people around them
will have a strong impact on their direct work environment and eventually on the wider organization they are part of. However, energizing leadership initially is about what those leaders do, the behaviours they show
and the engagement and commitment they create in the organization to
make things happen. The culture will be a long-term result of this.

We will come back to the issue of culture and climate when we consider section 8 (in Chapter 13).

Energize – engage – commit

We have already emphasized that we believe leaders should put more energy into mobilizing the people they work with. Peter Drucker made the point elegantly when he was talking about the shift from manual work and manual workers to knowledge workers. With the increasing levels of education around the world, the human talent available for work is almost without bounds. Drucker asks whether organizations are using to the fullest extent the talent available to them and whether they are offering ways of working that stimulate people to give the best of their abilities. His (and our) answer to this question is 'no', and we believe that one of the most important leadership challenges for the coming years is to find new ways of unlocking the human potential that is still hidden in contemporary organizations.

In the last decade of the 20th century, business HR leaders gave a high level of attention to performance management and the application of various performance management tools. Their aim was to achieve greater clarity regarding the mutual expectations for the job and creating higher levels of output.

Our employees seem to have understood this, perhaps partly because of the influence of the New Economy in the late 1990s and the numerous dot.com business initiatives. Our leaders, however, may not have understood this quite yet. Although the majority of those dot.com initiatives may no longer exist, the entrepreneurial spirit that came with them still does exist. And so does the feeling of freedom associated with working in small start-up businesses – and the realization that every person in such organizations needs to perform at a high level right from the very start.

Research by the Career Innovation Group showed clear evidence in its report *Riding the Wave* of how young professionals' attitude to work and their career has changed. The 'performance contract' obligations are better understood, but in turn expectations regarding the work that organizations offer today have become more critical. The same applies for the willingness to stay with one organization beyond the current job, which has diminished.

Case study: *Riding the Wave: The new global career culture* (Jonathan Winter and Charles Jackson, Career Innovation Group)

The Career Innovation Group is an alliance of global companies (including Boeing, BT, GlaxoSmithKline, Marriot, Nokia, Pfizer, UBS) whose ambition it is to create a culture of enterprise, a sense of purpose and a high-trust 'career partnership' with talented people. Their goal is to be seen as inspiring companies.

The 'Riding the Wave' project involved an external panel of 1,000 young high-flyers from 73 nations in an internet-based study to better understand their career aspirations and to find out about their experience at work.

These high-flyers have established an employment relationship in which they offer self-managed performance in return for good experience and the trust of their employer. But the 'performance contract' contains a serious flaw. Companies are failing to deliver many of the things that young professionals value most and, as a result, 40 per cent of them say they will leave their present company within two years. Only 7 per cent expect to stay for another five years or more, and 73 per cent have recently been approached about another job offer. They take a short-term approach to careers, riding the business waves – from hot trends to network opportunities to skill development options – in an effort to gain greater employability, financial rewards and personal growth.

Given the link between staff retention, client retention and the bottom line, the potential damage to businesses is incalculable. Companies wanting to retain this young cadre of future leaders will have to create a corporate culture that is attractive to this critical workforce, and a 'development contract' based around a succession of 'development waves'.

If possible, these waves should include an international assignment at an early stage; 98 per cent are willing to accept work abroad, and the more they experience living away from their home country, the more they like it. They also need help with career planning and personal development, and better information on internal job openings. If they receive it, all this development and career planning will be sure to make them more employable. But the paradox is, according to the Career Innovation Group research, that making people employable will actually encourage them to stay with their current employer.

In outlining six steps that companies should take, the report calls for much more than a resurgence of best practice in career development. In order to survive, large employers need to make a radical shift away from traditional thinking about what it means to be a member of an organization. Instead, they need to build more diverse and explicit career partnerships with different individuals and groups. Some will be short-term partnerships with non-core workers or independent consultants. Others will be long-term arrangements with a core team of relationship-builders.

Companies that can strike this balance will have created the flexibility they need, together with a new kind of stability in the workplace – stability based not on job security for all, but on diverse choices, strong personal relationships and shared values.

Some leaders understand the new challenges better than others and adapt their leadership to new insights. They understand that the organization can only benefit from higher levels of engagement of the people around them. It is amazing to see how some organizations can improve their performance by raising engagement levels. We have seen this happen in various organizations. The business they were in did not change fundamentally, and the workforce stayed largely the same. The only change was a change of leadership and a different behaviour from the new leader compared to that of the previous one.

PART THREE

Case study: The leader makes a difference

A food business in the Netherlands with net sales of 280 million euros and 1,100 employees had been missing its targets three years in a row and was gradually losing momentum. The business was still profitable, but the level of profitability was falling and the sales growth slowing. Compared to sister companies in other European countries, the business became a mediocre performer, running the risk of dropping to the bottom of the peer group in Europe.

In late 2000 a new, young leader was appointed. One of the first things he did was to organize a workshop with the leadership team to work out a vision for the business, to clarify the strategic priorities and to build the team. The workshop was a combination of physical outdoor activity and a series of dialogues and sessions to get the work done. The new leader was very open about what sort of person and leader he was and about the way he wanted to work. He made himself vulnerable by putting his cards on the table before the others did. The team members were invited to do the same, and they responded positively to that. There were some emotional moments when people opened up and expressed their deeper hopes and fears. The workshop was a different event from the various management meetings that had taken place under the previous leader. The team came out of the session with the new leader with renewed energy and a strong team feeling and commitment. In addition, some difficult choices regarding the future of the business and the strategic priorities had been made.

The new leader and his team members used every opportunity they had to talk about the way forward for the company and to stress the importance of getting everyone on board for the new strategy and the new way of working. The new leader made it very clear that he wanted to be held accountable for success or failure. He wanted to receive immediate feedback from anyone in the company if his behaviour as leader was not in line with what he and the leadership had communicated and set out as the way forward.

The latter was crucial. People understood the message and responded to it. They did provide feedback, in a spontaneous and candid manner. The new leader had struck a chord, revealing that constraints and frustrations existed in the organization, but also opportunities and lots of energy and initiatives to make things better. What he had managed to do was not only to convince the organization about the strategic direction he wanted to take it in, but also to create an emotional buy-in from the people involved at all levels.

To prevent a gap between the leadership team and the wider management team from emerging, another workshop along the lines of the first was organized in early 2001 for some 30 people. This was also intended to prepare the wider management team for the challenges that they were going to face in the changing environment. Again the programme was set up in such a manner that both the rational side and the emotional dimension were addressed. The outcome was very positive, although not every individual could buy into it. For those members of the team, counselling took place and solutions were found.

The above story continued, and many more activities were undertaken to enhance the engagement of people at all levels and to create deeper commitment for what needed to be done. This started at the top, but was continued on the basis of a well-structured programme engaging broad groups of people.

It turned out to be a winning strategy. Confidence within the company was growing rapidly; a lot of energy was released and was directed to efforts to improve the performance of the business on the market. The results in 2001 and 2002 were improving rapidly. The risk of joining the bottom pack of peer companies in terms of business performance was reversed; instead, the company found its way up again. The confidence of the European leadership team in the capabilities of the Dutch food business was restored, and visible signs of this growing confidence were a tangible token for the people working in the Dutch food business that they were on the right track.

The results of the people survey in 2002 showed a substantial improvement compared to 2000 on practically all dimensions.

PART THREE

Connected leaders

Let us look at a number of possible scenarios for leaders who decide to invest in higher engagement of the workforce.

If the leader decides to focus on informing people about the strategic direction and explaining the vision and strategic priorities in a rational way at various levels only, he or she will get rational confirmation of the chosen direction (or not). The emotional buy-in, however, will fail, and this will show in the execution. The performance will be average, or slightly better than average.

If the leader decides to focus on clear strategic direction and getting strong commitment from the organization at different levels, it depends on the sort of leader whether or not this is going to be successful. If he or she is a technocratic, rationally oriented person, we would argue that this approach will be difficult. This person will not have the capability to go out to the wider organization successfully and convey the key messages. Even if the CEO attempts to do this, the result will not be positive. Employees in today's organizations are well educated and informed, and they know and understand what needs to be done to improve the performance of the business. A CEO who behaves smartly to get rational buy-in will fail in the eyes of today's employees and will not have the credibility to inspire people within the organization. The minds will be touched, but the hearts of the people will not.

If the leader is a holistic and authentic person, the attempt to engage and commit wider groups of people in the organization will be successful. There is a sharp distinction between leaders with the traditional skills and competencies set who focus on rational arguments for getting their ideas across, and the more modern leaders who combine this capability to get buy-in for the 'what' with less conventional methods and approaches.

For a company to be successful, in any case a structured approach needs to be in place to cascade the leadership an organization wants to have. The above case of the Dutch food business is a clear illustration of how this can work successfully.

Higher engagement levels work, but need to be sustainable in order to create real commitment. This is an important statement, and crucial for how energizing leadership will lead, or fail to lead, to mobilization of the workforce.

A one-off event with the top leadership team may have a positive impact, but will not embed the new leadership behaviours and approach.

In his book *The Connected Leader*, Emmanuel Gobillot says that real leaders are connected leaders. Old leaders are formal leaders. They are diplomatic, tactful, managerial, efficient, knowledgeable, expert and credible. Real leaders, by contrast, are innovative, risk takers, approachable, warm, communicators, listeners and flexible. They have a different language and offer a different mental map.

The impact of those real leaders is magnetic, says Gobillot, and this new kind of leadership is necessary to get people to follow the leader. To achieve this, real leaders do three things. The first is that they connect through trust. They are aware that they have to build credit on their trust account before they can spend any. The second is that they align through meaning. They talk with individuals about their purposes and how those individual purposes can mesh with the purpose of the organization. In that way they align the real organization with the formal organization. The third is that they sustain through dialogue. They tell stories instead of being evangelists.

We will come back to the statement that higher engagement levels work, but need to be sustainable in order to create real commitment, under section 8 ('Create a winning organizational climate'), which is dealt with in Chapter 13.

Leadership and accountability

Leadership in local and independent businesses back in the 1980s was relatively straightforward. The local company would decide the marketing and sales strategy, would decide the sourcing and manufacturing strategies (owning their own factories), would have their own R&D organization and would have their own finance and HR strategy.

By the early 1990s the picture was changing rapidly. Marketing and branding strategy was starting to be decided at regional, if not global, level; sales remained local for the time being, but one of the first areas that was exploited for cross-border synergies was the supply chain.

Large, international organizations all had to respond to the changing business environment and new ways of working. Regional roles and teams were established, with different scope and responsibilities. Many organizations were eventually forced to redefine their operating framework and create truly regional or global structures for some processes (brand equity management, the supply chain). The paradigm of strong local organizations having full command over their business changed rapidly in the late 1990s. Local companies that had once been successful and powerful in their own territory had to reposition themselves as parts of larger regional, international chains of interdependent units.

In the area of finance and HR, some early initiatives to achieve cross-country synergies could be observed, but apart from at companies like Hewlett Packard, IBM, British Petroleum, etc, this did not gain real momentum.

All of the above has led to a situation in the past two to three years in which many large international organizations have held on to parts of the old concept of independent local companies, while creating and putting in place regional or international frameworks. As a result, many organizations have become fuzzy. Roles and responsibilities have become diffused. Duplication of effort has become the rule rather than the exception, and decision making has become increasingly difficult. In such an environment it becomes increasingly difficult to identify who is accountable for what, and hence difficult for a leader to hold others accountable.

The situation described is one that is very unhelpful for energizing leaders. They want to get on with things and have a clear mandate. They want to be able to empower others to do what needs to be done in the interest of the entire organization.

We believe there is a strong case to be made for clarifying roles and responsibilities in modern organizations, for making bold choices in this context and for clarifying and communicating the operating framework. In this way, energizing leaders will be able to provide a clear platform to work from, to establish a clear system of delegation and corresponding accountabilities at various levels in (their part of) the organization.

Speed up execution

The above may come across as a fairly negative description of how large international companies have operated in recent years, but we believe it to be the rule rather than the exception.

In such an environment, aligned and coherent implementation of decisions becomes rather cumbersome. In large, complex international organizations the implementation of any decision through 1,000 or more geographically dispersed managers is a nightmare.

Energizing leaders, however, do not take the given situation for granted. They quickly identify what the scope of their job is, and the decision-making authority connected with it. The next step they make is to clarify and communicate this to their leadership team and the wider organization, and make it understood. By doing so, they focus their own energy and that of those around them on what they can really do and achieve. This is a liberating process both for the leader and for others.

A special concern of energizing leaders is to clarify for themselves primarily what their responsibilities and accountabilities are. They themselves find it impossible to work in a fuzzy environment. Therefore, they put a high level of energy in the early days of their assignment into creating the right framework to operate in.

They do so in full awareness that having the right framework is vital for a powerful, speedy and successful implementation of any decision. In particular, the issue of speed is important to them. In today's world, response time can be an important competitive weapon.

Probably energizing leaders are not fundamentally different from other leaders as regards their wish to create an environment in which decisions can be made quickly. The difference lies in the relentless effort energizing leaders will put into sorting out what needs to be done to improve the situation. It is not the words but the deeds that count.

Dealing with increasing pressures and complexity

Peter Drucker questioned whether organizations are using to its full extent the talent available to them and offering ways of working that stimulate people to give the best of their abilities. The answer to this question is often negative, and we believe that one of the most important leadership challenges for the coming years is to find new ways of unlocking the human potential that is still hidden in contemporary organizations.

We observe a growing tendency in the corporate world to respond to rapid change, globalization, new technologies and the complexity coming from these by turning to conventional leadership and management methods. Many leaders attempt to manage this increasing complexity through 'clear' and 'strong' leadership from the top, and simplified top-down approaches. By doing so, they expect to be able to re-establish stability and predictability. In today's world many of them will fail.

It may be very tempting to tackle complexity by using models and frameworks from the top down so that complexity is brought back to a level of simplicity that can be managed easily. The risks of this leadership approach to increasing pressures and complexity are obvious, in our view. Managers and employees will in the end perceive only the parts of the reality that fit with the frameworks and guidelines given to them. Other parts of the changing reality in consumer behaviour, customer expectations, external developments, etc may easily be overlooked. Can you imagine what consequences this may have in the longer term?

Rather than creating detailed rules and procedures to manage complexity, it will be important in international, matrix-based organizations to learn to deal with complexity at various levels, including across borders. Clear processes may help to allow rapid decision making.

Rather than creating detailed job descriptions to manage the complexities of modern organizations, it will be important to have a good understanding of key roles and responsibilities and how they fit with the overall operating framework.

Apart from the philosophical aspect raised by Peter Drucker – that human potential in such organizations is greatly underutilized – the engagement levels in day-to-day work will suffer, new business opportunities may be overlooked and innovation capabilities will be reduced. Eventually it will become difficult to retain talent in such an environment.

We should strive to create and nurture organizations that are passionate in their desire to achieve the opposite: human capital and talent is given the space and room to manoeuvre quickly when action is required to grasp new business opportunities; people are empowered to respond to challenges since they know best what is required for successfully managing them in their day-to-day work and to do this in the most efficient manner.

A key leadership task to make such organizations function well is to ensure that everyone understands the direction the organization wants to go in, and the key activities underpinning this strategic direction. In other words, the leadership task here is to ensure engagement through a shared vision. In a modern organization this is coupled with the leadership capability to engage people not just with their mind, but also with their heart. It is this combination that we believe will bring renewed energy to organizations and will create sustainable competitive advantages.

We will come back to the importance of a shared vision and shared values for creating emotional and intellectual engagement in section 3 (Chapter 8).

7

Section 2: Build the team

> **Build the team**
>
> - Do we have a deep understanding of our members and their strengths and weaknesses?
> - Do we use this understanding to create genuinely balanced teams?
> - Is the legacy that team members have left behind in previous roles in line with the team requirements?
> - Are the ambitions of individuals known and supported by the team?
> - Is the team capable of renewing existing practices?
> - Do the team leadership and climate stimulate diverse opinions and views?

Introduction

'Build the team' should not be confused with team building. In section 6, 'High-performing empowered teams' (Chapter 11), we will discuss the relevance of team building. In this section we want to focus on the importance of carefully crafting the (senior) leadership team for any organization. The word 'crafting' already suggests that this is not a one-off effort that an organization makes. Building the team is a dynamic process and requires ongoing attention and decisive action from the top leadership.

With our choice to focus here on leadership teams we are limiting ourselves, since many other sort of teams exist, such as project teams, coordinating teams, expertise teams, support teams, etc. Our choice of leadership teams is a logical one in the light of the previous section ('Energizing leadership to mobilize people', Chapter 6) and in the context of the following sections. Leadership is the red thread running through all the areas we are addressing.

For a proper definition of leadership teams we need to clarify what a real team is. We will use the definition that Richard Hackman of Harvard University presented in a leadership development conference in London in 2003: 'a real team has a collective task that demands a high level of interdependency among its members, something that can only be accomplished together; and clear and stable boundaries, so that membership is not constantly changing, and it is easy to tell who is on the team'.

In this chapter we will focus on the last part of this definition, where it says that team membership should not constantly change and that it should be easy to tell who is on the team. Who is on the leadership team – 'who is on the bus', in Jim Collins's words – and who should leave the team and who should join the team is clearly the responsibility of the leader.

HR has a dual position. On the one hand, the HR director is normally a member of the leadership team, but also acts as adviser to the CEO as regards making changes to that same team and for proposing activities that will further develop and strengthen the team as a whole, and its members.

Leadership development

HR in large international organizations has traditionally focused on individual leadership (or management) development: the development and supply of the 'right' leaders for the 'right' jobs at the 'right' time. Many organizations have programmes in place for competency development, so that the future leaders are well equipped for the challenge they may face in future jobs. In combination with succession planning, possible successors for key positions can be swiftly identified once a key position becomes vacant. The resulting 'big picture' regarding availability or unavailability of appropriate candidates also gives a sense of direction for leadership development programmes to be organized, so that skill and competency gaps can be filled.

The above process fits with organizations that follow the principle of 'promotion from within'. We believe this philosophy to be the preferred one, since it allows the people in the organization to grow with the business and since it provides a healthy degree of continuity. This does not imply that in all cases internal candidates should be appointed. A good portion of external recruits is necessary to create the right mix and balance and to provide skills and competencies that may not be readily available within the organization.

In the above way of working, a number of pitfalls should be avoided:

- Taking a specific position in a leadership team for granted in terms of responsibilities and role in the team, and concentrating on swiftly finding a successor for that position, could be risky. Doing so may overlook opportunities for rebalancing the overall team and the available skills, competencies and experience among the other members of the leadership team.

- The identification of a candidate for a position in the leadership team is sometimes based on a more generic assessment of 'successful' performance in the past. The risk is that a thorough analysis of a candidate's real track record in the light of the requirements for a future role does not take place.

- In many large international organizations the above way of working leads in practice to an expectation that for successful career progression, regular job changes at relatively small intervals are the norm. This can easily lead to a lack of leadership continuity and accountability.

We will address each of the above three issues in turn.

Dynamic position profiling

When a vacancy in a leadership team arises, this offers a unique opportunity to rebalance the overall team and to optimize the mix of available skills, competencies and experience. This should certainly not be understood as a plea to constantly change each and every role and each of the team members. Rather, it should be seen as an opportunity to reflect the evolving needs of the organization in the composition of the leadership team and its members.

An example: a business that has gone through a major acquisition and merger programme in a volatile competitive environment may want to use a vacancy for the finance function to reinforce the importance of internal functional excellence in finance, instead of placing a heavy emphasis on negotiating deals with other parties. Also, the profile for the future finance director may require more of an 'integrator' type of person than an aggressive 'go-getter'. The implications of the changes in the profile of the finance role need to be looked at carefully in the light of the overall team composition.

Another example: an organization that has gone through a heavy restructuring programme on the manufacturing side of the business may ask itself how a successor to the technical director can be focused more on providing technical support to the innovation programme in support of the marketing strategy. This will probably lead to a very different profile for candidates for the technical director role.

These examples may seem obvious, but it is sometimes surprising to see that organizations do not use the flexibility they have regarding the definition of the role profile and the profile for candidates to fill the job.

One tends to assume that the departure of one of the members of a team is necessary in order to trigger changes to the overall team. We do not believe that this is right. 'Building the team' implies that the leader continuously checks whether the balance of the team is right and whether the team is fit for purpose. Assuming that a leadership team stays together for a minimum of four or five years, it is likely that the leader will need to make changes during the course of this period, without changing the team members. The core part of the individual roles may stay more or less unchanged, but there may be a need to assign a new assignment or strategic project to one of the members of the team.

A good illustration of this is offered by UBS, the Swiss bank.

Case study

In June 2004 the senior management team at UBS started a project to look at how the financial services business would evolve over the next five or six years. That exercise led to several conclusions. First, the amount of money flowing into hedge funds and other so-called alternative asset classes would continue to grow. Second, managing money for very wealthy individuals would be a global business.

These insights led to a remarkable reshuffle at the bank, which was announced in June 2005. John Costas, the chief executive of UBS's successful investment bank, announced that he would leave his current job and would take charge of a new in-house hedge fund.

Peter Wuffli, UBS chief executive, said that the move would allow UBS to offer its own hedge fund-type products to institutional and private clients. It also would allow UBS to hang on to its most talented traders, who were continually leaving to join other hedge funds.

The move of John Costas was questioned, since he, as the deputy chief executive and as a successful builder of UBS as a force in investment banking in the United States, could have been a candidate for bigger jobs than building up the new in-house hedge fund for UBS. However, Costas insisted he was mainly motivated by building up a new business more or less from scratch and that there would be greater levels of investment in alternative asset management vehicles for UBS in the long term.

This example illustrates the point that it is likely that the chief executive of a top leadership team will need to make changes to the allocation of individual tasks and responsibilities during the lifetime of a team, without necessarily changing the team members. This stresses two points. The first is that the CEO needs to have a clear view on the track record of individual team members: their skills, competencies and experience. The second is that the CEO and individual team members need to have the courage to think out of the box and need to have the capability to develop solutions, as UBS found when a new in-house business (a hedge fund) had to be set up.

We see it as a key responsibility of the CEO to carefully craft the top team as described above. We will come back to the importance of time in job. We believe that continuity in the top leadership team is important for success.

Importance of talent management

Hay Group in the United Kingdom conducted a survey of 400 senior HR and business leaders. The results revealed that although most HR directors and business leaders agreed that their companies viewed talent management as a 'high priority' (61 per cent), they had grave concerns that 'the board' did not fully understand how it impacted on their business.

If people play the largest role in company success, how is it possible, then, that according to the survey fewer than one in ten organizations have a clear picture of the capabilities of their people? And how can it be that for more than half of all businesses, according to the same survey, talent management appears on the boardroom agenda less than twice a year?

Internal talent reviews have become increasingly important over the past few years. Faced with tighter budgets and a more uncertain business climate, companies have become more risk-averse over the past decade. Businesses want people with experience of the same market, and preferably even the same company, at the top. This situation has become more acute in a climate where people tend to move between companies, often spending as little as two or three years in a job before looking to move on.

To help establish talent management practices, companies need to identify the DNA behaviours that predict success across their organization. These DNA behaviours are unique for a particular organization; they are based on the organization's 'genes'. They reflect how things are accomplished successfully in that organization and how business success is achieved. Business leaders need to work out how their people link back to business strategy. It is vital for companies to start focusing on the precise understanding of what it takes to succeed in different roles. World-class talent management is about getting this alignment and role definition right.

Once this planning is in place, it is vital to conduct regular talent reviews of the people in the organization and their capabilities in order to establish an overall talent 'big picture'. By doing this, companies can make the best use of their people. Having a fuller understanding of their capabilities and how these can be used to drive business strategy will help to increase success.

Track record and time in job

A survey using the checklist of www.newHRagenda.net among 72 participants in the 2005 European Clients Meeting organized by Hay Group revealed that only half of the respondents say that their organization has a deep understanding of its team members' strengths and weaknesses. Even fewer actually use this to ensure that teams have a balance of skills, competencies and experience. The score on the latter was the lowest of all items in the 56-question checklist!

It seems that we readily say that people are the most important asset, but that we do not often invest in proper processes and systems to capture their skills, competencies, experience, successes, etc. This questions the accuracy of information that is used for selection decisions and thereby also the accuracy of appointment decisions.

This problem is potentially worsened if the organization has a culture in which people move from one job to another rather quickly and do not stay longer in a specific job than two or three years. In this sort of environment the building of a track record as such becomes problematic. At the more senior levels in an organization we assume that it takes a minimum of three years before the results in a specific job become visible and can be properly assessed.

In his book *Good to Great*, Jim Collins makes a plea that top leaders need much longer than three years to steer an organization to success. He is arguing that leaders of businesses need a longer tenure in the job to come to a full understanding of a business's competency, to reach an effective judgement on the company's future strategic direction and to form a perception of what the key factors are in managing a successful execution of this strategy.

In the light of the above, Jim Collins doubts whether 'celebrity CEOs' can be successful. Often they arrive under pressure to perform quickly and deliver success, and by focusing on doing so they run the serious risk of failing to understand what the real competency and success factors for the business are. On the people side the same issue occurs. A quick rational analysis of what needs to be done does not necessarily guarantee a successful execution of the new strategy, and certainly does not ensure a deeply felt commitment from larger parts of the organization.

Jim Collins has expressed his views on the above topic by stating that CEOs should first decide who is 'on the bus' and who is 'not on the bus'. In a way, he is paraphrasing the paradigm that 'People come before vision and strategy'. We believe that the reality of businesses forces us to be pragmatic about this. In some situations an immediate decision needs to be made about the departure of a member of the most senior team, and an immediate successor then needs to be found. In other situations it may be wiser to continue to work with the existing team and its members, and to build the team in a more evolutionary way.

There is a tension between time in job and continuity on the one hand and renewal and diversity on the other hand. Sticking to the same team and its members for too long could become a negative factor when it comes to diversity that stimulates innovation. We will come back to this in section 6, 'High-performing empowered teams' (Chapter 11).

Section 3: Shared vision and values

Shared vision and values

- Is there a written statement of what the vision is?
- Has the vision been elaborated with a larger group of people?
- Has the vision been communicated to everybody in the business?
- Are the values aligned with the vision?
- Are surveys used to check how well the values are being lived?
- Is the application of variable pay (bonuses) consistent with the vision?

Introduction

Many organizations have carefully crafted vision statements. Normally these explain why organizations exist, what 'business' they are in or want to be in, who the key stakeholders are, what the strategic direction for the organization is and how success will look. Sometimes mission statements are used next to a vision statement or to replace (part of) the vision statement.

However, many other organizations do not have explicit vision statements yet. This does not necessarily mean that no vision exists, but if the vision is not properly prepared, decided and shared, it is difficult to see how larger groups of people can benefit from the sense of direction provided by a properly communicated vision. Therefore, we would argue that a vision statement is a must for large international organizations.

The benefits of a shared vision are even greater. Elaborating a vision and a vision statement with a larger (but not too large) group of representatives of the leadership is in itself a rewarding process. Certainly this is the case when this activity is combined with the use by individual leaders of focus groups, reference groups, functional teams, etc to support the process of elaborating the vision or parts of it.

Another feature of a shared vision is that careful thought is given to how the vision can best be communicated to the wider organization. This communication process should in principle cover all levels. For different levels in the organization the vision should be communicated in a different form and shape, but all levels deserve to be informed about the vision.

Shared vision and engagement

We believe that one of the key differentiating factors for the coming years will be the degree to which organizations create a higher level of engagement of employees in the organization. We have already clarified this in section 1 ('Energizing leadership to mobilize people', Chapter 6). We define engagement as the extent to which employees commit to something or someone in their organization, how hard they work and how long they stay as a result of that commitment. Engagement has a big impact on the performance of the organization and on the ability of an organization to retain talented employees.

A shared vision definitely helps to raise the level of engagement. This is particularly the case if the shared vision is combined with the concept of organizations doing business successfully but also meaningfully. The latter includes an active, external engagement of businesses and employees with the environment and communities they operate in.

The two – external engagement and winning the hearts and minds of employees internally – often go hand in hand. The combination of focused deployment of strategic business choices together with emotional engagement at all levels in the organization provides alignment and accountability! We believe that this can be a winning formula for the coming years.

Case study: Ben & Jerry's

A good example of a company that combines its vision for that business with a 'social mission' is Ben & Jerry's, the Vermont ice cream company.

Ben & Jerry's was founded by Ben Cohen and Jerry Greenfield in 1978. They started to develop, make and sell natural ice cream made from Vermont dairy products in an old gas station in Burlington. Their concept of natural ice cream made from Vermont dairy products became a big success. The business rapidly developed into a regional business and eventually Ben & Jerry's became a very popular brand throughout the United States. Today Ben & Jerry's ice cream is famous around the globe.

The vision of the two founders of Ben & Jerry's was that business is one of the most powerful forces on earth and that 'business has a responsibility to give back to the community'. They declared their dedication to the creation and demonstration of a new corporate concept of 'linked prosperity'. The Ben & Jerry's mission consists of three interrelated parts: a product mission, an economic mission and a social mission:

- The product mission is to make, distribute and sell the finest-quality all-natural ice cream and related products in a wide variety of innovative flavours made from Vermont dairy products.
- The economic mission is to operate the company on a sound financial basis of profitable growth, increasing values for shareholders and creating career opportunities and financial rewards for the employees.
- The social mission is to operate the company in a way that actively recognizes the central role that business plays in the structure of society by initiating innovative ways to improve the quality of life of a broad community: local, national and international.

PART THREE

Underlying the mission is the determination to seek new and creative ways of addressing all three parts, while having a deep respect for individuals inside and outside the company, and for the communities of which they are part.

Throughout its existence, Ben & Jerry's has had a strong focus on social justice and equality, eliminating negative impact on the environment and giving back to the communities where Ben & Jerry's does business. So far, Ben & Jerry's has lived up to these expectations and has managed to integrate its commitment to values into its day-to-day operations wherever and whenever possible.

The fact that these are not just hollow words is illustrated by the many projects and initiatives that Ben & Jerry's has undertaken over the course of time, for which part of the profit was made available. Those projects and initiatives include supporting the 'Global Warming Campaign'; the 'PartnerShop Program', which helped unemployed people to set up new Ben & Jerry's outlets; an environmentally friendly resourcing programme, 'Native Energy'; and thousands of small, local initiatives to deal with local social issues.

Ben & Jerry's reputation has been built on the wonderful ice cream it sells, but more importantly on its values-led mission and the numerous concrete initiatives it has been part of to bring the vision, and in particular the social mission, to life. Ben & Jerry's has not built the brand through million-dollar advertising campaigns!

It is obvious that working in a company like Ben & Jerry's requires a strong commitment to the mission. The feel and touch of the organization are special. The Ben & Jerry's philosophy is also kept alive through the 'Ben & Jerry's' factory tour in Waterbury, which is one of the most popular tourist attractions in Vermont.

We have said that one of the key differentiating factors for the coming years, in our view, will be to create a higher degree of engagement of employees at all levels in the organization, combined with the concept of organizations doing business in a meaningful manner. The latter includes the active external engagement of businesses with the environment and communities they operate in. We gave Ben & Jerry's as an example of how this can be done successfully.

There is no doubt that there is still an enormous reservoir of untapped human potential. A greater external involvement and engagement with the environment and communities we operate in will help to unlock this potential.

Peter Drucker has convincingly pointed out that, despite the revolution from manual worker-centred organizations to knowledge worker-based businesses, we are still far from fully utilizing the human capital in organizations. He is right. Optimizing the utilization of human potential will require us to create more meaningful organizations and jobs.

A paper titled 'Sustainable leadership' from the Career Innovation Group relates that there is a high level of awareness of the importance of 'community, social and ethical issues'. An emerging theme is that people in organizations seek to make work more meaningful and to feel that they are contributing to the community in some way.

There is increasing evidence, both from the Career Innovation Group's research and from research generally, that people are looking to their organizations for meaning, context and a way of making a wider contribution to society. However, the number of companies that see this as an important issue is still relatively small.

Linked to the above is the way in which ethical issues seem to be handled within organizations. All see ethics as an important issue; nearly all are giving it prominence through values statements and codes of conduct. In some cases it is also addressed on leadership development programmes.

The role of values

Some recent crises in renowned international organizations (Andersen, Enron, WorldCom, Ahold) have raised the question of how we can avoid such catastrophes and build successful and meaningful organizations for the future through higher levels of trust and integrity. We believe that those organizations that come up with a quick and appropriate answer to

PART THREE

this challenge will be able to position themselves best and will be able to attract and develop the best human talent. Doing so will require higher levels of (intellectual and emotional) engagement combined with clear strategic business choices, and we believe that values play an important role in this.

The case of Enron shows that values need to be fully understood by the top leadership to start with and that the behaviours of top leadership need to be aligned with those values. Only then can trust and integrity become real and only then will the values be understood and lived by the great majority of workers in an organization.

Enron, at the time of its fall, had a professional values programme in place. Enron had developed its values, had a values statement in place, had a programme to communicate the values to the wider organization, had organized promotional activities to support the values programme, had banners setting out its values, and so on. The issue was that the leadership behaviours were not aligned with the values. With hindsight, we now know that one of the main reasons for the collapse of the business was the behaviour whereby management developed practices that led to high rewards on the basis of business deals and revenues that were not properly accounted for.

Enron is a clear example of how important values are, and a warning of what can happen if they are not aligned with leadership behaviour. However, done properly, values statements can be the glue that keeps the different parts of large international organizations together. It is necessary to start by developing a clearly articulated vision and set of values, which must then be disseminated and made understandable at all levels of the organization. Maintaining the company's vision and values, consistently communicating and living them across locations and within all units, over time, is an important leadership task and will have a big positive impact on the climate in a company.

All this assumes that the vision and values are relevant to and respectful of local cultures worldwide, which in our view speaks for itself. Moreover, we must stress once more that it is crucial that the visible (leadership) behaviours are in line with written vision and values statements and the communication around those.

Another point that needs to be emphasized is the importance of keeping the values alive over time. A one-off effort with no proper follow-up could, over the long term, worsen the situation rather than make it better.

We see a huge strategic challenge for business HR to help businesses to find the right way forward in this context. HR can make the values explicit, but, more importantly, should monitor the company's actions to ensure that leadership behaviours are aligned with those values. If this is not the case, HR should intervene and agree appropriate action with the top leadership to remedy the situation. The Ben & Jerry's case shows that it is possible to integrate a commitment to values into the day-to-day operations of an organization.

Trust and integrity

Stephen Covey, author of *The 7 Habits of Highly Effective People*, predicts that more scandals like Enron will occur. He may well be right. In summer 2005 the former CEO of WorldCom was sentenced to 25 years in prison, after he had been found guilty of an $11-billion fraud.

Stephen Covey is clear that the traditional leadership approaches and management tools will not be good enough to survive in future. Top-down leadership, in his view, will not work. Some of the existing management layers in large international organizations need to disappear, and he believes that tight control systems will fail. These practices are a thing of the past rather than the future. They are based on a lack of trust, and Covey believes that trust and integrity are the keys for successfully mastering the challenges that lie ahead of us.

He also uses the Peter Drucker argument that traditional leadership in today's world treats the well-educated workers of today in an inappropriate manner. He argues that moral leadership is required in order to create an environment in which the workers of today are willing to give the best of their abilities to the organization they work for. This moral leadership should aim for a situation where employees trust each other and focus on the things that they know are most important for doing a successful job.

Leadership involves setting the direction for what employees need to focus on, and stimulating engagement to make this happen effectively, on the basis of the principles that have been set out for the strategic direction of the organization, for the way that people are expected to work together and for the values that are felt to be important.

Covey believes that modern leadership is primarily about credibility and integrity. These are prerequisites for building trust at all levels in an organization. Without this, honest communication will be difficult to get, and emotional engagement will not exist. He sees the building of trust as the most important challenge for organizations in the 21st century.

Trust and betrayal

In recent times there have been a series of high-profile situations where business leaders have acted questionably. The greater pressures and pace of change have helped to create these situations. However, when the chips are down, some leaders inspire trust in their stakeholders through their consistency in holding to their beliefs and through their strength of character, whereas others do not manage to do this. The leaders who do inspire trust do so by being clear about their own and their organization's values.

Michelle Reina, co-author of the book *Trust and Betrayal at the Workplace*, has pointed out that there can be a wide range of situations where a breach of trust or the perception of a breach occurs, intentionally or unintentionally. The case of the WorldCom CEO is clear enough, but many other situations occur where the borderline between acting in a way that honours trust and acting on the basis of something other than trust is blurred and not so straightforward. These situations include, for example, restructuring resulting in lay-offs, delegating without authority, not keeping agreements, and giving and accepting performance targets that are unrealistic.

We foresee that leadership decisions and behaviours in relation to values and integrity will become even more important in coming years. We see a clear need for helping modern leaders to develop the capabilities required for establishing trust throughout organizations on the basis of personal credibility and integrity. The success of this will depend on how they deal with minority dissent in teams, how they organize delegated criticism and how they create a culture with open and honest feedback.

Use of surveys to check the pulse

Good companies do regular people surveys at two-year intervals and act upon the results of the survey. We believe that this is not good enough, given the emergence of some of the leadership issues described above. We would argue that there is a clear need to do 'pulse checks' in between the two-year large-scale people surveys, focusing on a limited number of critical leadership issues. The urgency exists, and nothing should stand in the way of organizing regular checks more frequently with the help of modern technology.

Case study: Marriott gains more value from its annual employee opinion survey

Marriott wanted to ensure that its global people survey met the needs of all its properties worldwide – but in an easy, employee-friendly and non-bureaucratic way. The company has been able to manage its global surveys in an efficient manner, enabling management leaders to spend more time analysing the results and taking action to address issues.

Marriott's Associate Opinion Survey is conducted annually, involving over 1,300 Marriott properties worldwide and upwards of 150,000 associates. In this process, a significant challenge is determining and responding to the requirements of participating properties.

In response, an innovative 'help desk' website was created to provide round-the-clock support to Marriott staff assisting with the effort. The site contains a highly detailed 'frequently asked questions' list that is both organized by topic and searchable by keywords. These FAQ resources allow survey coordinators to find solutions to the most common survey issues immediately.

By making the survey process easier for the organization to manage, the 'help desk' website gives Marriott more time to focus on what is really important: using survey results in an effective way so as to drive organizational improvement.

We need to have a human measure for how leadership in a particular organization is doing, alongside the financial measures and feedback offered daily by stock markets. Organizations that have embarked upon regular 'pulse check' surveys to monitor the perception of leadership and leadership behaviours are not widely spread, but nevertheless we believe that those organizations are in the forefront.

The same applies to organizations that have embraced the use of 360-degree or multi-source feedback systems. These tools and systems, we believe, provide very useful feedback on (leadership) behaviour and help to establish a climate in an organization that brings the best out of its people.

9

Section 4:
Strategic framework

Strategic framework

- Are there just a few clear strategic priorities?
- Have these been communicated in a compelling and inspiring manner to all key stakeholders?
- Are strategic priorities translated into concrete and tangible actions?
- Is it clear what the programme for key innovations will be?
- Is there overall sufficient level of ambition in the business objectives and plans?
- Is there a process in place for the rapid reallocation of resources in the event that specific business activities are terminated?

Introduction

Strategy development and strategic planning have received a high level of attention in the past 15 years or so. This was all done in an attempt to prepare better for the future and future challenges. No doubt many organizations have benefited from a more structured approach to strategy and strategic planning.

In recent years there has been growing awareness of the fact that some of the well-thought-through, rigorous strategic planning approaches have not been able to foresee how external forces would impact on organizations over a period of 5–10 years. In addition, strategic planning activities have sometimes focused on 'doing more of the same', instead of exploring new opportunities outside or adjacent to existing ones, on the basis of the real competencies available in the organization.

A framework

Every strategy statement and strategy development process must have a number of components. It needs a framework.

The organization must be clear about where it stands in the sector or industry it is part of. This must always be set against the environment the organization is operating in, or the one in which it wants to operate in the future.

A strategy statement must explain how the organization intends to be successful against the competition. It must clarify how the organization is going to be better and faster than the competitors and different from their rivals. The ambition level for the future needs to be defined and it must be clear what the organization is going to do differently in future in order to be (more) successful than in the past. This also needs to be translated into a financial framework that provides the critical performance indicators for measuring future performance and success.

The challenge these days is not to simply benchmark a competitor's products and imitate its methods, but to develop an independent view about tomorrow's opportunities and how to exploit them. Hamel and Prahalad have pointed out that path breaking is much more rewarding than benchmarking. Path breaking requires hard work, rigorous processes to develop strategy, creativity, courage, and an extremely good knowledge of the available competencies in the organization.

Jim Collins also emphasizes the importance of a deep understanding of what it is that the organization is passionate about, what drives the economic engine and what the organization can be the best in the world at. It is only on the basis of this deep understanding that organizations can create breakthrough strategies.

Strategy into action and aligned variable pay practices

A necessary first step in the process of making a strategic framework intellectually understood is often to translate it into more tangible and concrete actions. We call this process 'strategy into action' (SiA). Most modern companies have some sort of 'strategy into action' approach in place.

SiA normally starts with the formulation of a vision or mission statement that carefully reflects the essence of the strategy or the desired change in strategic direction. This vision or mission forms the basis for a limited number of strategic thrusts. A more modern terminology is mustwin battles. Strategic thrusts or must-win battles underpin the strategy by capturing the vital objectives that the organization must achieve in order to survive and be successful. Each strategic thrust or must-win battle is further worked out and specified in terms of key activities and key actions that must be undertaken to execute the strategy successfully. And finally, critical performance indicators are formulated to measure progress and success (or failure).

By including various stakeholders and by covering various management levels in an organization, a relatively high degree of alignment can be achieved. The risk of such SiA approaches is that the process becomes too bureaucratic. However, if this is avoided, SiA is a useful tool.

HR can see to it that the SiA process is properly organized and understood. The outcome of the SiA process can be used to define work plans for individuals and teams that are truly aligned with the strategy. This would include an aligned work plan for the HR team itself.

Another responsibility for HR is to design variable pay or bonus systems that are also aligned with the strategy. If both the work plans and the variable pay system are aligned with the strategic framework, this becomes a powerful combination.

Unfortunately, in reality this alignment often does not exist. We would argue that the design or the redesign of the variable pay system should more actively be looked at than is done normally. Basically, every strategic review should be followed by a review of the reward practices, particularly for the variable part of reward. A proactive approach from the HR side can add real value to a more rapid and better execution of the strategy.

Compelling communication

Many organizations publicly state what their strategy is or will be, how they intend to execute it, what the measurements for success will be, etc. If companies do not actively pursue these aims themselves, financial analysts and others will draw their own conclusions and measure the company's performance against them.

Some companies have been struggling in the past 10 years or so with the rapid increase in demands regarding expected transparency and openness towards the outside world regarding strategy and strategic direction and objectives. Such demands have sometimes led to situations where an organization communicated its strategic direction to the external world first, before doing so internally. That is the wrong order.

We do not argue that the key messages should be delivered simultaneously and in the same manner both externally and internally. Delivering the messages in the same manner can lead to a situation in which the same strategy statements and PowerPoint presentations as were shown to shareholders and financial analysts are also used internally to get the message across. This may work for a few people in the organization, but it will certainly not be understood by the vast majority of employees.

It is fascinating to see how sometimes within a relatively short time-frame new buzzwords emerge or particular phrases become fashionable and frequently used. That in itself is great, but it is problematic if it happens without there being a proper definition or understanding of those phrases and without their having a real meaning. Probably every reader can think of at least two or three examples, such as 'We will give high priority to operational excellence', 'We want to beat the competition', 'Fit for growth', 'Be better in what we do', 'We want to be the best in innovation'. And so on.

These words and phrases may be all right in themselves, but it is crucial that it is understood what they mean in more tangible terms and what is expected from the people in the organization to make

> them come true in the daily work. We cannot stress enough that this process of operationalizing the strategy requires hard work and time. HR can add value by putting in place a process by which work planning is done efficiently.

'Must stops'

In many organizations, people have the feeling that they are being overloaded. Announcing the outcome of a strategic review and launching new initiatives to underpin the new strategy tend to create a perception that the workload is going to grow further, rather than a perception that the result will be a more focused set of priorities. To some extent this can be countered by looking explicitly at those activities that need to be stopped. We call these 'must stops'.

'Must stops' are necessary in order to create the space for other new activities and to free up the energy needed to work on the newly determined priorities. Communicating explicitly which programmes and activities will be stopped will encourage people and teams to review their own set of activities and priorities and to align their new work plan with the new strategic framework. The outcome of the 'strategy into action' process will give clear guidance for the things that need to be done in order to execute the chosen strategy and its 'must-win battles'. This 'to do' list can well serve as a checklist for the things that should go to the 'must stop' list.

Another way to achieve the above is to use so-called golden rules. These rules give guidance to how things need to be done in a certain organization (for example, 'don't start a new initiative before having completed or stopped another one'). Many HR departments would definitely benefit from a disciplined 'must stop' process and from 'golden rules'. Specifically, in organizations where different parts of the organization are not fully aligned and have undertaken many different initiatives that all require support, a 'strategy into action' and 'must stop' programme can help to streamline the activities, and raise a clearer profile of HR and the contribution that can be expected.

In summary, it is important for any organization to have a clear framework setting out how it wants to become better and faster than its competitors and different from its rivals. The ambition level for the future needs to be defined and it must be clear what the organization is going to do differently in future in order to be (more) successful than in the past.

10

Section 5: Aligned and lean organization

Aligned and lean organization

- Are the targets and work plans aligned with the strategic priorities?
- Is the organization structure aligned with the strategic priorities?
- Are organizational processes aligned to deliver the strategic priorities?
- Is the average span of control at least 6?
- Is the average revenue (output) per manager higher than in comparable organizations?
- Is the number of management layers smaller than in comparable organizations?

Introduction

Alignment is a word that is often used in modern organizations. Taken literally, its meaning may be too static to describe what the process of alignment in organizations implies.

When we speak about 'aligning the work plan with the strategic priorities', we mean much more than just repeating the strategic priorities as part of the work plan and adding some further information and nice words to it. What is necessary includes acquiring a full understanding of the strategic priorities and their background. It requires that meaning be given to the strategic priorities in the context of the environment that a business unit is operating in. It requires that specific key activities underpinning the strategic priorities be defined, worked through in more detail and prioritized.

When we look at the process of alignment in this way, it becomes a more dynamic activity, involving and engaging larger groups of people at various levels in the organization. This process may be initiated from the top, but it is clear that there is an important bottom-up dimension to it as well.

Organization structure and strategic priorities

Structure in relation to an organization is like anatomy in relation to the human body. The structure defines how assets and resources are distributed over the organization and how roles and responsibilities are allocated (rather as in the case of bones, muscles, the head, the feet, organs, etc for the human body).

There is no such thing as the one and only right structure for a particular organization. It is essential, however, that the organization structure is designed in such a manner that it allows the organization to execute its strategic priorities successfully. In other words, it is important that the structure is aligned with the strategic priorities.

Case study: Vishay Intertechnology: 'One Face to the Customer'

Vishay Intertechnology is a manufacturer of active and passive electronic components. With a turnover of approximately $3 billion and 27,000 employees worldwide, Vishay continues its growth strategy by acquiring and integrating other companies. Within the past 10 years, Vishay has completed six major acquisitions.

In realizing the company's 'One Face to the Customer' strategy, one of Vishay's biggest challenges was to define a generic matrix structure that allows easy integration of past and future acquisitions. An approach for analysing interaccountabilities within management was introduced, and is now implemented in all Vishay's business units and at all its geographical locations. The benefit of this exercise was that it clarified decision-making processes, which improved efficiency and reduced the number and significance of power games.

The generic approach to structuring allows Vishay to make its business model explicit, and very clear to newly acquired companies. Moreover, the generic business model allowed the company to manage cost structures effectively and to improve performance by adding further management tools such as grading model and talent management.

If a company has a strategy of growing rapidly and gaining market share through a limited number of global brands, it is obvious that this company does not need to have brand specialists at local level. Rather, it will want to have a strong central team with superb brand development and brand communication marketers.

If a company is in the service industry and has a strategy of providing better service to its clients than its competitors can offer, it makes a lot of sense to have a strong ground force in place with excellent operators wherever needed.

If a company has as a strategic priority fundamentally lowering the cost of its product(s), this organization may want to have a central team in place for the procurement activities and on the supply chain side for the most cost-efficient allocation of production volumes over different factories. On the other hand, the same company may choose to have strong local factory managers so that they can successfully manage local cost-efficiency programmes, restructuring, employee relations, etc as part of the wider supply chain network.

The number of examples is almost unlimited. In every situation the important thing is to create organization structures that enable an organization to execute its strategic priorities successfully.

The examples already mentioned illustrate that excessively dogmatic choices with regard to organization structure will not work. Too often, discussions around the design of organization structure tend to be black and white. The choice should not be to have either a fully centralized structure or a fully decentralized structure. As in the example of the company that needs to lower costs, the choice may be to have a centralized buying team and supply chain team for the allocation of production volumes, but decentralized factory managers who are part of the wider supply chain network.

Another superficial contradiction is suggested when discussions in large international organizations focus on having either a fully nationally based organization structure or a fully globally or regionally based structure. Some parts are best organized nationally and some others globally or regionally. Coca-Cola will want to manage its product formula and brand strategy at global level, whereas the availability and visibility of Coca-Cola in the shops are managed locally.

The Unilever ice cream business is a good example of an organization that needs a combination of:

- global innovation programmes and transfer of knowledge;
- regional supply chain efficiencies;
- local responsiveness and flexibility.

In our experience, it is important for large international organizations to ask which capabilities are required in each of those three areas: innovation and transfer of know-how; efficiencies to raise the level of competitiveness; and responsiveness and flexibility. This will give some good first indications of how the organization structure should be designed.

The answers to these questions may differ depending on the industry or sector you are in. Generally speaking, the chemicals industry will require a much greater degree of global integration than the packaged foods business, whereas the cosmetics business may be in between.

In our experience, it is a useful second step to think through the role of the operating (business) units 'on the ground' that deal with suppliers, customers, consumers, clients, etc. Too often they are treated on a 'one size fits all' basis. It is important to assess the relative strength of each of the units and the relative strategic impact they have. This assessment could well lead you to decide on different strategic roles for different units, and this may require different solutions in terms of organization structure.

Being lean and benchmarking

Organizations have become increasingly complex, and therefore it is not surprising that a loud call for simplification can be heard in many organizations. Some leaders go so far as to say that complexity should be brought down to a level of simplicity. We do not believe that this can be done. We believe that organizations should work in such a way that unnecessary complexity is avoided and that the remaining, unavoidable complexity is managed effectively.

Some organizations have developed their capability to manage complexity better than others. Single-point accountability helps people to be clear about who does what and who decides what. Having fewer management layers shortens lines of communication and reduces the number of interfaces and interface issues. A proper system of delegation brings the authority to decide at the lowest possible level in the organization, which speeds up the decision-making process.

Benchmarking becomes important to compare one's own organization with others, so that opportunities for improvement can be identified and realized. Within large international organizations the opportunities for internal benchmarking are a logical first step. Depending on the organization's ability to pick up the learning from one part of the organization and transfer it to another part of the organization, internal benchmarking can deliver substantial benefits.

Comparing organizations and how they work can be done by using metrics, but we believe that informed conversations between professionals are needed in addition, to make it possible to understand differences between parts of a larger organization, why some things work well in certain circumstances but not under other circumstances, etc. However, we make a plea for measuring those aspects of organizations that can be measured properly. In the checklist, we have chosen the following three measures, since these can be applied generically across organizations:

PART THREE

- *Number of management layers*: having too many layers hinders communication and stands in the way of deciding and acting with speed.

- *Average span of control*: research has shown that high-performing organizations have relatively high spans of control (more than 10 direct reports to a manager, whereas for averagely performing organizations the span of control is more likely to be in the range of 4–6). The high-performing organizations stretch their spans of control by delegating appropriately, having high-calibre people, using a clear operating framework, etc. Higher spans of control allow a reduction of the number of management layers. For example, a large organization with a management population of say 1,000 and an average span of control of 5 needs five management layers. If the same company had organized itself to be leaner and better and had created an average span of control of 10, it would need only four management layers.

- *Average revenue per manager or employee* (for a non-profit organization, revenue should be replaced by the key outcome produced by the organization): in the case of the Unilever ice cream business, revenue per manager or employee differed by a factor of 5 between the lowest-scoring unit and the highest-scoring unit. Some of that difference resulted from objective differences in economic environment, currency movements, etc, but the fact remains that differences existed that could not be explained by objective factors and that could not be influenced by those units.

Work plans and targets

In section 4 (Chapter 9) we have already discussed the importance of having a clear strategic framework. Leadership has responsibility for the development of strategy and for the creation of work plans and action plans throughout the organization. The better the alignment between the strategic plans and the work plans for units, departments and individuals, the greater the chances are that the organization will be able to deliver on its goals and targets. We pointed out that the use of 'strategy into action'-type processes is an important tool to create such alignment.

Given the fact that work plans and targets in many organizations are linked to the variable pay system, there is also a reward implication. Well-aligned work plans and targets can be expected to have a positive effect on reward and the perception of reward systems, in particular the variable pay system. Badly aligned work plans and targets can be expected to have a negative effect.

Building broader organizational capabilities

For an organization, being aligned with its strategic priorities represents an important organizational capability. The same can be said for having the right quality of people in key roles, developing talents and having a well-filled talent pipeline. These are areas where HR can add value to the business.

Case study: Standard & Poor's: developing more integrated services

Standard & Poor's is one of three major global credit-rating agencies. The credit issuer and investor market segments that the rating agencies serve have been changing rapidly; they are requiring more integrated services from the agencies and the development of more self-sufficiency in credit analysis.

Standard & Poor's strategy was to meet the evolving market requirements, but the agency faced a significant challenge in that its organization structure and supporting systems (eg reward and capital deployment) were based on a profit and loss operating model. An analysis of Standard & Poor's strategy and organization, carried out using a series of diagnostic tools, showed that this strong profit and loss model encouraged internal competition rather than collaboration. This finding led to a redesign of the organizational structure to address misalignments identified during the analysis.

> The result of the project was a new structure that removed a barrier to, and enabled, true top team collaboration. The client gained an organizational structure and job requirements consistent with its strategy. The structure and job requirements enabled the development of competencies that were used for executive assessment, selection and development. The integrated organization redesign and competency-based assessment gave Standard & Poor's the basis on which to create a high-performance top team, something that had previously eluded it.

Other areas where an important contribution can be delivered through the people side to create aligned and lean organizations are:

- *Skills enhancement and training.*

- *Creation of learning networks or communities of practice.* Especially in large organizations, the capability to pick up learning from one part of the organization and transfer it to another part can have an important impact on the organization's ability to grow and innovate.

- *Establishing a culture of teamwork.* In an interdependent organization, teamwork is essential to get work done effectively.

We will look at these aspects in more detail in the next section.

11

Section 6: High-performing empowered teams

High-performing empowered teams

- Are multifunctional teams in place for the priority activities?
- Do those teams have clear briefs signed off by the leadership team?
- Are the teams truly empowered to deliver results?
- Do those teams have the right tools to perform their tasks?
- Is there formal training to accelerate teamwork?
- Is there a process for systematic review of required team skills and competencies?
- Is the leadership competency model being used to drive winning behaviour?

Introduction

In sections 3, 4 and 5 we looked at the importance of having clarity about the shared vision and values and about the strategic priorities, and an organization that is aligned for an effective execution of those priorities. We stressed that compelling communication at various levels in the organization is vital.

If we assume that all this has been done successfully, what then are the next challenges? What capabilities are required to make things work in the best possible manner?

In section 2 ('Build the team', Chapter 7) we talked about carefully crafting the (senior) leadership team for an organization, long-term leadership development and talent management. This work represents an important capability area necessary for a successful performance.

Another capability area, and one that we will address in this section, is 'High-performing empowered teams'. Every organization has teams; some even argue that teams have become the most important building blocks of organizations. The question we want to focus on in this section is how the effectiveness of teams can be improved so that average teams become high-performing teams.

There are some new insights with regard to effectiveness of teams, in particular diverse teams, and the importance of this for the team's capability to innovate. We will spend a fair share of this section on that specific topic, since we believe that there is a challenge and an opportunity for HR to contribute to a better-performing organization.

Before we do so, we want to have a look at some other important aspects of teamwork and well-performing teams in general.

Teams develop

Teams develop over time, and therefore teams at different stages of development may look different to the outside world. This does not necessarily mean that a team that still has a long way to go to become a high-performing team is a bad team. Other teams that have been together for a longer period of time may show good teamwork as such, but may have reached a level of performance that they will not be able to further improve on. They will never become a high-performing team.

Bruce Tuckman, in his article 'Developmental sequence in small groups', has provided a useful model to identify the stage of development of a team:

- *Forming:* the team members come together and the team is built.

- *Storming:* a rather chaotic phase where differences of opinion and styles come to the surface and team members will be inclined to prioritize their own interests.

- *Norming:* the members of the team are beginning to accept the role they are expected to play in the team. The team develops its rules and way of working. Interdependencies are becoming more important.

- *Performing:* the team is more important than the individuals. There is a confidence that the goals can be achieved. The team members complement each other's work and show mutual trust. The leader creates the right conditions for the team's work.

We would add to Tuckman's model:

- *High performing:* the team delivers results and receives recognition. The team is inspired by this. On the basis of trust, the team members accelerate their personal and collective learning, which further enhances performance.

Successful teams add value

Successful teams effectively turn strategy and goals into tangible actions and results. They make decisions more rapidly and create support for their decisions in the wider organization. They adapt faster to changing market conditions or to changes in their organization. This obviously leads to better results.

There seems to be consensus about some key conditions that make a team successful:

- **Clear, engaging and meaningful direction.** Challenging goals that are relevant for the organization motivate teams. The clarity needed for successful teamwork implies that there is a clear orientation and empowerment given to the members of the team for what they are supposed to do. In order to achieve such clear, challenging goals, all the available talent has to be engaged.

- **Empowered team structure.** A real team is bounded and stable over time. The team members need to work interdependently to reach their common goal. They are empowered to manage their own teamwork and their internal processes. They develop their own norms of conduct ('What must always be done and what must never be done'). There is support from the wider organization that the team works in.

- **The right team composition.** The ideal size for a team is six to seven people. Often, teams are too big. The team members need to have integrity with regard to the team. Individual team members need to have the right skills and competencies. Regarding the latter in particular, the competencies connected with emotional intelligence (self-awareness, integrity, empathy, influencing others, etc) are of great importance.

Beside the factors mentioned above, it is important that there is support from the wider organization. This support is twofold. First there is the moral dimension. Without visible support, especially from the leadership team, it will be difficult for a team to perform successfully. The team must be empowered to make its own decisions, within an agreed framework and mandate for the team.

Case study

Teams need support from the wider organization. In an international pharmaceutical company, tensions existed between the board of directors and one of the divisions. The main reason for this was that the board and the divisional director had differences of opinion about the strategic direction for the business, resulting in poor cooperation and lack of trust.

Within the division the divisional director and his team chose to go their own way, resulting in the board recalling and changing decisions made by the division, without consulting the divisional leadership team. As a result of these interventions the members of the divisional team felt they were not taken seriously. The situation worsened and finally the divisional director resigned.

His successor had the difficult task of restoring the confidence of his team. He realized that the support of the board would be of critical importance. After several discussions with the board, the mandate for the divisional team was clarified. The board publicly expressed its confidence in the divisional team and the new leader, and consistently communicated its trust in the divisional team to other parts of the organization.

The second aspect of organizational support is material support. This includes the availability of appropriate information systems, a stimulating physical working environment, but also a fair assessment of the performance of individual team members and the team as a whole, coupled with a fair reward based on that assessment. We also want to stress the importance of the availability of training to accelerate the building of teams and to provide guidance for developing teams into high-performing teams. This is an area for capturing the learning from successful teams, identifying what works best in the organization and making this learning effectively available to others in the organization by designing, organizing and executing relevant training programmes.

International and global teams

In recent years, many organizations have embarked on a journey towards international ways of working. In the chemicals industry and the steel industry, this process started early, in the 1970s and 1980s, because of the nature of the business and its client base. Others followed, with the fast-moving consumer goods industry joining later, in the early 1990s. Today, it is hard to imagine how large corporations could survive without this international dimension.

> More recently the trend towards internationalization has become even stronger and is now called globalization. Icon brands like Nike, Coca-Cola, Pepsi, McDonald's, Toyota, BMW, Microsoft, Cisco, General Electric, Sony and many others show that consumer needs around the globe are converging and that those companies would not survive without a global approach, organization and mindset.

What then is a global organization? We said that teams are perhaps the most important, key building block for any organization. If so, what do global teams look like and how should they best organize themselves and develop themselves into high-performing global teams? These are challenging questions for people who used to work in well-protected national companies, with clearly defined rules of the game, operating in a clearly defined geographical area where all employees, customers, consumers, etc speak the same language.

As regards what we said above about the development of teams, the conditions for becoming really successful as a team, or possibly even becoming a high-performing team and adding substantial value to the business, all apply to international or global teams as well. For them there is an additional challenge, and that is to make this all work for teams that manage businesses across an international region or worldwide. Almost by definition, these teams need to be composed of people from diverse background, in terms of nationality, language, education, etc. What is the nature of this additional challenge?

We should remind ourselves of Bruce Tuckman's model to identify the stage of development of a team:

- *Forming:* the team members come together and the team is built.

- *Storming:* a rather chaotic phase where differences of opinion and styles come to the surface and team members will be inclined to prioritize their own interests.

- *Norming:* the members of the team are beginning to accept the role they are expected to play in the team. The team develops its rules and way of working. Interdependencies are becoming more important.

- *Performing:* the team is more important than the individuals. There is confidence that the goals can be achieved. The team members complement each other's work and show mutual trust. The leader creates the right conditions for the team's work.

We added to Tuckman's model:

- *High performing:* the team delivers results and receives recognition. The team is inspired by this. On the basis of their trust in each other, the team members accelerate their personal and collective learning. This further enhances performance.

Even in the first development stage – *forming* – it becomes evident that international or global teams have some additional challenges to cope with compared with natural teams from within one company and country. The physical coming together of the team members is more complicated and, even more importantly, recruitment and selection of the right team members require the organization to have a solid and well-organized talent management system and process. An important task is to organize the talent management efforts effectively on a global scale, so that the business knows where leadership talent exists, who is available for international moves, who should be challenged to play a substantial role in the global arena, who should attend high-profile leadership events, etc. We believe that relatively few global businesses are in good shape in this respect and that a lot still needs to be done to arrive at a stage where doing global business is supported by effective global HR policies, processes and systems.

In the second stage of team development – *storming* – it becomes even clearer that it is difficult to organize international and global teams around apparently straightforward business priorities. A representative from an Italian food company will find many reasons why it is impossible to work together with a knowledgeable food manager from the United States. This stage of team development is very clarifying, maybe even purifying, until the reasons why the individual members are part of the team and what is in it for them are sorted out. The time that the team members spend together in this phase can be quite confusing. However, if the team survives and finds a common way forward, the foundation for becoming a high-performing team has been laid.

In the next phase – *norming* – a more professional approach to becoming a successful and high-performing team takes over. The team members acknowledge that different cultural orientations exist, but they decide to overcome the differences. The role of the team leader is extremely important in this stage. The team leader does not impose a way of working on the team members, but rather lets them come to an agreed way of working. Given the differences of cultural background, disagreement could easily occur. The team leader in this phase needs to let the team do its work, but to intervene effectively when seemingly unbridgeable differences of opinion are starting to stand in the way of teamwork.

In the fourth stage of development the team really starts to perform and deliver result. This is probably an easier phase in the development of the team, since the initial barriers for becoming a real, successful team have been overcome.

Effective teamwork, diversity and innovation

Above we have elaborated on the additional requirements for becoming a successful, high-performing international or global team, compared to the requirements for a natural team operating within a well-defined geography with limited complexity. Recently, extensive research has been done to identify the key success factors for successful teamwork. In particular, the researchers examined the capability of teams to innovate successfully. It turned out that, first, diversity within teams and, second, the way in which issues are dealt with and decided upon play a crucial role.

Track record and time in job

Our survey using the checklist among 72 participants in the 2005 European Clients Meeting organized by Hay Group revealed that only half of the respondents say that their organization has a deep understanding of their team members' strengths and weaknesses. Even fewer actually use this to ensure that teams have a balance of skills, competencies and experience. The score on the latter was the lowest of all items on the 56-question checklist!

It seems that we readily say that people are the most important asset, but that we do not often invest in proper processes and systems to capture their skills, competencies, experience, successes, etc. This questions the accuracy of information that is used for selection decisions and thereby also the accuracy of appointment decisions.

The problem potentially is worsened if the organization has a culture where people move from one job to another rather quickly and do not stay longer than two or three years. In this sort of environment the building of a track record as such becomes problematic. At the more senior levels in an organization we assume that it takes a minimum of three years before the results in a specific job become visible and can be assessed properly.

Depending on the nature of the teams, an upfront judgement needs to be made about the required duration of the assignment for each of the team members. Sometimes compromises will have to be made, but we need to realize that changing the jobs of individual members of the team too quickly can have a very negative effect on the performance of the team overall.

In this section we focused on how the effectiveness of teams can be improved, so that average teams become high-performing teams. We looked more specifically at international teams and the effect of time in job.

In the next chapter we will look at coaching and the role that coaching can play in improving the performance of individuals, teams and the organization as a whole.

12

Section 7: Coaching: develop yourself and others to win

Develop yourself and others to win

- Is there a clear definition of 'talent development', a definition that is understood by most people?
- Is it clear what support line managers can give to help improve individual performance?
- Are individual targets clear and seen as stretching but achievable?
- Is it well articulated how 'coaching' can contribute to a better leadership style?
- Has this organization a stimulating coaching culture?
- Have board members and other key people received training in coaching?

Introduction

There are too many different sorts of coaching and coaching activities to describe here. In principle all of them may be right, as long as they serve the purpose they have been designed for.

In recent years, coaching has received a lot of attention. Many organizations are looking at ways to get more out of the efforts that leaders and managers are putting into 'coaching' their team members.

At the higher levels in organizations an individual form of executive coaching has become fashionable. Over a longer period of time an executive has one-to-one conversations with his or her external coach. In these conversations the executive, with the help of the coach, has an opportunity to reflect on the work and, in retrospect, the way in which the executive handled different situations, and to look ahead at future challenges. These conversations may lead to the identification of competency gaps and agreeing actions to fill these gaps. It may also lead to trying to better understand the deeper motives and drives of a person in the light of the job that a person holds and finding a more authentic and effective leadership style to master the challenges coming from the job. Frequently, finding a better balance between working and private life also becomes part of the executive coaching agenda.

This form of individual and intense personal coaching has been known for many years in the world of sports. Famous sports personalities and teams almost without exception have famous coaches. Although the coaches do not always appear in the spotlight of the publicity surrounding top sportspeople and teams, they play a crucial role in bringing them to outstanding levels of performance.

Top performers in the world of entertainment have also adopted these practices, well known from the world of sport. The most famous singers and movie stars even have more than one coach to support them in different areas of life: to improve their technical skills in singing or acting, to keep them healthy and in good physical shape, to advise them how to present themselves in public, to manage the business side of their career, etc. Some of these practices have also found their way into business life, but are restricted to a very few CEOs who can afford to organize such an infrastructure around them to support them personally in improving their performance.

We do not underestimate its importance and power, but in this section we will not focus on that type of coaching. Rather, we want to explore coaching approaches that help to improve leadership and leadership styles in larger organizations. If a leader becomes more effective, the team members will improve their performance too, and ultimately the whole organization benefits from higher levels of performance throughout.

Find a common definition

HR can add value by helping organizations to develop a clear definition of what specifically is expected from coaching activities to be undertaken and the overall coaching approach to be taken. There is no one right solution. It is important to understand the current reality of the organization and the stage of development, so that an effective coaching programme can be designed to take the organization to the next level.

The common element in our view should be that the coaching activities are designed with the aim of creating and producing results through people. In large organizations, leaders and managers want the members of their team to be successful. As 'coaches' they want their 'players' to be successful, and more successful than in the past. They want their players to win at their goal. Such coaching programmes have some common features.

First of all, they should improve competencies within the organization for individuals to develop themselves and to develop others. Individuals and organizations that have excellent competencies in this area perform better overall. The process starts at individual level, where a passion to develop oneself continuously lays the foundation for personal growth and success. If individual leaders manage to achieve high levels of self-development, it is likely that they will also stimulate the people they work with to develop this competency in themselves. Eventually this becomes an important factor for success in the wider organization.

We argue that it is best to put a structured programme in place to help leaders and their teams to work on the competency to develop themselves and others. This can be done through central workshops, or train-the-trainer types of approaches, or through individual competency development activities. Depending on the current reality, each organization should find the most effective way forward in this respect.

Second, successful coaching programmes should enhance coaching capabilities as a key building block of leadership and leadership capabilities. It is fair to expect an organization to articulate clearly how coaching can contribute to the sort of leadership that the organization desires. If an organization wants or needs a leadership philosophy that does not include the coaching dimension, it would be foolish to invest in developing coaching capabilities. However, we see a strong link between the desired energizing leadership as described in section 1 (Chapter 6) and the capabilities that an organization has for coaching. We see this as the right way forward for virtually all modern organizations.

Third, successful coaching programmes are used to build a winning spirit and culture. The search for continuous improvement at individual and organizational level becomes an important value of the organization. If a person wants to be successful, that person must work on his or her own development and that of others. That is the way the organization wants to work, and that is what is expected from the people working or aspiring to work in that organization.

We are assuming here that trust and teamwork are other values that are important in that organization. Only in a climate where trust and teamwork are the rule rather than the exception will people feel free to work effectively and wholeheartedly on their own development and, particularly, on the development of those around them.

The importance of training in building a coaching culture

It is our experience that successful coaching programmes start with a formal training activity. This allows the organization to make it clear what a coherent approach to coaching looks like (see the three points mentioned above), and it is a clear signal that the organization is serious about this initiative, wants to invest in it and is determined to make it a success. Coaching becomes part of the culture.

Good initiatives at individual level or at a lower level in the organization run the risk of not having sufficient impact and not being sustainable in the long run. We believe that it is more effective to target a bigger organizational unit or group of units and have them go through a formal training programme.

This approach has a number of other advantages. It makes it possible to train natural teams. Those teams can swiftly integrate the newly acquired coaching insights into their day-to-day leadership behaviours. This is probably the most productive way to disseminate those behaviours to the wider organization.

Also, this way of working makes it possible to build relatively quickly the critical mass in the organization needed to make the initiative stick. It avoids situations whereby individuals are trained away from their daily work, so that when they return they find themselves in a situation where their new skills and improved coaching competency do not resonate with the rest of the organization.

Another advantage is that having a larger-scale training activity means that some of the people trained at the start can be asked to act as coaches for other colleagues later in the programme. We have seen programmes where this became a powerful feature of the training. Initially trained 'coaches' with some real, new coaching experience were asked to play an active role in helping new 'coaching graduates' in the two months immediately after the training workshop to apply, practise and improve their coaching activities in their daily work. They acted as a sort of help desk and catalyst for bringing the learned coaching skills and competencies to life.

Finally, successful training programmes for coaching cater for the fact that as far as behaviour is concerned, people have different styles of reacting to the circumstances and situations they encounter. It is crucial to recognize that each style has its strengths and weaknesses; no style is better or worse than any other style. Sometimes, however, those different styles create problems, since we see other people through the filter of our own predominant style. Our style has an especially important effect on the area of our interpersonal relationships and communication with other people. If we want to be effective, we must learn to modify and adjust our own predominant style to meet the needs of others. A good understanding of these differences is vital when it comes to coaching. Effective coaching requires that we develop the capability to manage people's different interpersonal styles flexibly.

Coaching competencies and performance management

Normally the building of coaching skills and competencies from the point of view of the one being coached (the 'coachee') follows a couple of stages. In the more initial stage the coachee is gaining experience of how coaching works, when to ask for support from the coach, and so on. The coachee practises in normal work and further develops the skills and competency to coach others.

The most powerful stage occurs when the coachee sees the benefits of the coaching approach and becomes fully committed to it. This is the stage where new ways of behaving become visible, initially in the day-to-day work of the coachee, but also in the behaviour of the people around the coachee. This is a stage where new energy seems to emerge.

In this climate it becomes possible to stretch the efforts of the team to a higher level of aspiration. We found that there is important learning in terms of the sequence of things. If a leader and the team choose to raise their level of ambition too quickly, or if they are forced to do so by higher management levels, there is a serious risk that they will fail, or at best the improvements will last only a short time. The negative effects could easily be a falling back to mediocre or even worse levels of performance.

If the bar is raised more gradually once the leader and the team together have built their coaching capabilities, however, there is a fair chance that they will cope with the work challenges in a realistic and sound manner. The team becomes a winning team.

The above has an important implication for target setting and defining work plans in any organization. There is a tendency to increase pressure and sharpen targets if a business unit or a specific part of an organization is not performing well. Statements like 'If unit X performed better, our overall results would be better' may be correct in themselves, but we should not expect the performance of unit X to improve as a result of such statements alone. Instead of raising the expectations in terms of results for unit X, leadership should give priority to getting the team of unit X back into shape again, developing its members' capabilities to cope with the work challenges they are faced with and restoring their self-confidence, and only then raise the bar in terms of targets.

Instead of raising the targets for unit X, leadership should consider raising the bar in terms of targets for unit Y, which already performs well and has developed the capabilities to cope with challenges.

Coaching and inspiring conversations

Leaders and managers with good coaching competencies have a greater chance of having conversations with their team members that inspire performance. We call these inspiring conversations. Other types of conversations may have a strong impact as well, but we believe that a coaching style creates a climate in which barriers to higher performance are more likely to be removed.

Case study: 'The conversation gap: using dialogue to build trust and inspire performance' (Jonathan Winter and Charles Jackson, Career Innovation Group)

In 2004 the Career Innovation (Ci) Group set out to measure, understand and encourage effective conversations about trust, performance, development and success at work. The focus was mainly on the conversations that people have about their own work. The research was carried out through an international web-based survey supported by focus groups and individual interviews among high-flyers in six large international companies.

The good news from the survey is that conversations are plentiful and effective. In particular, managers are doing a good job. Despite the changing shape of workplace relationships (eg project-based working, virtual teams and matrix management), it is 'my manager' who remains the focus of most dialogue.

On average, people reported valuable conversations in the past 12 months with their manager on 6 of the 12 topics listed in the survey. Next in line are work colleagues and friends and family, each with 3 topics.

It is worth noting the overwhelming dominance of conversations with managers. For 10 out of the 12 topics, managers are the people talked to most.

Although people reported plentiful conversations over the past year, the Ci research identified a significant problem. Four in every 10 respondents said they still had a topic they would like to raise with their manager but had not done so. Ci called this the 'conversation gap'.

A closer look at the data reveals the huge impact of this gap. People with a topic they want to raise are less satisfied, less engaged and much more likely to be planning to leave. The issues that people want to discuss are individual and varied, but there is a recurring theme through the research: future-focused and development-focused conversations are being squeezed out by a lack of 'quality time'. The long-term invisible impact of this is substantial. Those with a topic to discuss with their manager are nearly three times as likely to be planning to leave their present employer.

The positive impact of good conversations is equally impressive. Satisfaction and engagement are both strongly impacted positively. Such conversations make people more motivated in their work, clearer about their work and career objectives, and more self-aware, and they feel generally reassured and valued.

The above research is relevant in the context of coaching capabilities, since it highlights that there are issues that may block performance, issues that could easily be removed through 'good conversations'. Leaders with good coaching competencies and skills are more likely to find the secret of getting results through their people by inspiring their performance. They succeed by taking a real interest, building trust and having regular conversations that are fully engaged in the individual's goals and concerns.

We explored coaching approaches that help to improve leadership and leadership styles in larger organizations. If the leader becomes more effective, the team members improve their performance too, and ultimately higher levels of performance will be found throughout the organization. In the next chapter we will explore how coaching, among other things, can contribute to establishing a winning organizational climate.

PART THREE

13

Section 8: Create a winning organizational climate

Create a winning organizational climate

- Is the leadership style genuinely seen as positive?
- Are surveys being used to measure progress regarding the organizational climate?
- Are successes being celebrated?
- Do people generally feel recognized for what they do?
- Are regrettable losses of people avoided?
- Can the organization attract the right people?
- Is the organization a good place to work in?
- Are the targets and the target-setting process generating positive energy?

Introduction

Most people would probably describe some of the southern parts of France and Spain as places with a pleasant, sunny climate. These are places that people want to go to, spend time in and enjoy. They are places with an interesting historical cultural background and contemporary cultural events. Everybody knows that these are good places, and when you go there you are in a mood of anticipation and are bent on having a good time. This reinforces the positive reputation of the places we are talking about. People become more and more committed to these places and may want to go there again, may want to spend their holidays there and possibly even buy a home and live there long-term.

If you replace the word 'places' by 'organizations' and the phrase 'spend their holidays' by the word 'work', you have a pretty good description of an organization with a positive climate, possibly even with a winning climate. We make a distinction between a positive climate and a winning climate. A winning climate is not just 'pleasant and sunny', but also radiates the feeling of ambition to be successful and to continuously raise the bar in terms of performance. It continues to develop itself and continues to embrace new initiatives that make sense. Continuously raising the bar in terms of performance is not based on pressure from the top, but is an intrinsic aspect of the behaviour of the people in such an organization. Raising the bar and raising the targets therefore is not seen as negative; rather, it creates positive energy in the organization.

In organizations with a winning climate there is a willingness to go above and beyond the call of duty, to 'go the extra mile', and this has a direct impact on the performance of the organization. Also, in organizations with a winning climate, people are likely to stay with the organization. These are two important benefits for organizations that succeed in creating a winning climate. Everybody who has worked in an organization with a winning climate knows how this feels, and how different it is compared to working in an organization where there is no such climate.

Leadership styles and organizational climate

If the climate is so clearly related to performance, and to the retention of people, it is relevant to ask what the key drivers of a positive and winning climate are. We know from research that various factors play an important role. It is important that the day-to-day work is meaningful, and recognized as such by others in the organization. It is important that the team of which a person is a member works well, has a clear sense of direction, has the right skills and competencies, shows integrity, etc (see section 6, 'High-performing empowered teams', Chapter 11). It is important that the organization does not interfere with how the work is done, but allows individuals and teams to do their day-to-day work in the way they know is best.

All of the above is important for creating a winning organizational climate. The key determinant factor, however, is the direct manager and the leadership style that the direct manager uses. This should not come as a surprise, but we believe that its importance is sometimes not fully realized.

There is no such thing as the one and only best leadership style; the challenge is to apply leadership styles that fit best with what is required in a particular organization. If it is done properly, there will be a positive impact on the climate within the organization.

Climate surveys

In the past decade or so, surveys have become increasingly popular. Their popularity started in North America, where feedback generally used to be more appreciated than in other parts of the world. However, with some exceptions, surveys in North America normally used to be limited to the management group and would not involve all employees and workers.

Case study: Improving employee motivation at Honda in the United States

Honda believed that creating a better work environment would boost results. Executives wanted to know, 'Are we as good as we should be? Do we have the right culture and climate? Do we have the right organizational structures? Do our people have the right capabilities for the roles they perform and are these right for the future?'

Honda has a major manufacturing plant in South Carolina. The plant management understood that creating the right kind of work environment would lead to better results – both for employees and for the organization.

A company plant-wide survey was conducted to gauge overall levels of engagement, and to identify opportunities to improve the organization's effectiveness. Business challenges included the difficulty of attracting and retaining key personnel, employee relations issues (eg absenteeism), and inexperience among the managerial ranks, along with other people-management challenges.

Based on the survey feedback, solutions were developed to address these key challenges. The business benefits of this work were:

- improved ability to attract and retain key personnel;
- increased front-line management training and capability;
- career ladders developed to clarify the roles and skills needed to promote talent development and long-term commitment of employees;
- the introduction of a new performance planning programme.

Europe saw a rise in the number of people surveys in the second half of the 1990s. The practice of using surveys was typically extended to a wider group of people at various levels in the organization. Initially the surveys tended to focus on employee satisfaction, but soon their scope was widened to include the measuring of additional areas that would give an indication as to whether an organization was functioning well overall.

Today we would say that surveys in one way or another have become a hygiene factor. Organizations that do not do surveys at all are missing an important tool with which to measure the effects of their decisions, behaviours and actions. Whereas, for example, finance professionals embraced surveys early on as a way to measure the reality, HR professionals took longer to become enthusiastic about what surveys could contribute.

Measuring the effects of strategy, practices and the overall climate in an organization can give invaluable indications of what needs to be done in order to improve the organization's climate and thereby to lay the foundation for a better performance. What really counts is the will that an organization has to find out what areas for improvement exist and to put decisive action in place to make effective changes for the better.

It is not the measuring as such that makes the difference, in our view. Sometimes large organizations tend to use survey results to create a sort of competition between the various internal parts of the organization. We do not believe that doing so is useful. It is much more important to get a deep understanding of the results for an overseeable unit, to identify areas for improvement and to agree actions to improve in those areas. It is this cycle of asking for feedback from various levels in the organization, doing something concrete to improve selected areas, asking for feedback, improving certain areas, etc that becomes a source of positive energy in the organization.

Feedback cycle

Organizations with a winning climate apply this so-called feedback cycle. People surveys are one tool that they use, but in most cases they will want to shorten the time intervals between people surveys, which at present are normally one and a half to two years.

There is a growing interest in organizing quarterly climate surveys with a limited set of questions and a smaller group of respondents. Other organizations have decided to use tailor-made monthly surveys to measure the effects of specific change programmes. There are many more possibilities for organizing all sorts of surveys relatively cheaply with the help of modern technology.

The essence is that only organizations that are passionate about performing better all the time carry out surveys of this kind. They are determined to find ways (including survey tools) to realize this ambition.

Feedback seems to play a crucial role in this. Some HR practices and systems have been redesigned to incorporate the 'feedback cycle'. Not surprisingly, this happened first in performance appraisal and perform-ance development systems. Whereas the more traditional systems were rather static and focused on one individual, the inclusion of feedback from people other than the line manager (other team members, project managers, functional peers in other parts of the organization, etc) gives a much more dynamic and holistic outcome. Such '180-' or '360-degree

PART THREE

feedback' or 'multi-source feedback' approaches are sometimes used as a key tool for realizing leadership change in an organization and for creating a different organizational climate.

The application of the 'feedback cycle' is especially relevant for developing the relationship between a team, its team members and the leader. We know that this is important for creating a positive climate to work in and for creating an engaged workforce.

Benefits of commitment

In section 1 ('Energizing leadership to mobilize people', Chapter 6) we made the point that building deeper levels of engagement and commitment in our view is a new leadership task and a key challenge for organizations for the coming years. Higher levels of engagement do work, but need to be sustainable in order to create real commitment.

> Inspired by the Corporate Leadership Council in the United States, we define engagement as the extent to which employees commit to something or someone in their organization, how hard they work, and how long they stay as a result of that commitment. The 'something or someone' can be the day-to-day work people do, the team they are part of, the direct manager or the wider organization they work in. In most cases it will be a combination of these four. The greater the extent to which people commit to this thing or things, the more they will be willing to 'go the extra mile' and the greater will be their desire to stay with the organization. These are very important benefits of higher levels of commitment.

Organizations with a winning climate do manage to achieve those higher levels of commitment. People feel generally recognized for what they do, and the organization is seen as a good place to work in. As a result, such organizations can attract the right talent and they can avoid regrettable losses of personnel.

The benefits described will be put at risk if the higher levels of commitment are perceived to be unsustainable. It will be interesting to learn from organizations that are in the forefront of the development of creating deeper levels of commitment how sustainability can best be achieved.

Some factors we have already mentioned. Leadership styles must encourage employees at all levels and not just those at the top to develop themselves and to contribute to the overall performance of the organization. Teams must be seen as a source of innovation and creativity. Diversity needs to be encouraged throughout the organization.

A threat to sustainable commitment occurs when organizations decide too frequently to reorganize the organization and the workforce. We observe that organizations with higher levels of commitment do not have problems in gaining acceptance for restructuring, provided the logic is compelling and has been well explained at various levels in the organizations. Modern employees understand that restructuring is sometimes necessary to keep an organization healthy, especially in certain industries. However, if the leadership uses the instrument of restructuring too often, in the perception of the employees, and if the logic cannot be or is not explained properly at various levels in the organization, there will be an immediate negative impact on the levels of commitment in the organization. As a result, there will be a negative impact on the ability of the organization to attract and retain talented people, and on the willingness of employees to 'go the extra mile'.

Next we will explore a relatively new but important factor for creating commitment.

Sustainable commitment through corporate social responsibility

Another important emerging factor for sustainable commitment lies in the area of corporate social responsibility (CSR). For many years, organizations have been expected to behave as good citizens in the communities in which they operate. However, these days organizations are expected to take a more proactive approach and to contribute actively to making

PART THREE

societies, and the world we live in, better. We mentioned the example of Ben & Jerry's in the United States as a company that has embraced this challenge in its social mission and supports, for example, the initiative against global warming, but there are many more companies today that actively support NGOs and other non-profit organizations. TNT is working actively together with the World Food Programme, and this has become an important internal binding factor for creating commitment in TNT units worldwide. Other organizations have adopted major initiatives to underpin the fact that they are serious about their corporate reputation and CSR initiatives (Philips, Johnson & Johnson, ABN Amro, McDonald's, Fortis, etc).

Those programmes serve another purpose, apart from the organization's own official mission and strategic objectives. The external stimulus and the 'do good' factor seem to cause the organization's employees to increase their emotional commitment. They feel that the organization they work for genuinely is a good place to be, and they feel personally recognized for this when they talk to family and friends about their work and what their organization does.

The future may well be that CSR becomes a major driver of a more fundamental redefinition of corporate purpose. The sheer existence of CSR as such becomes a hygiene factor for successfully doing 'business' long term – assuming that the existing corporate purposes are clear. On that basis, the organizations that are in the forefront will think through carefully, starting from their existing corporate purpose, which NGOs and other non-profit organizations they will want to work closely with. In future we may see UNICEF, Greenpeace, War Child, SOS Children Villages and many similar organizations finding their way to corporate offices and corporate executives more frequently.

We have made a distinction in this chapter between a positive climate and a winning climate. An organization with a winning climate continues to develop itself and continues to embrace new initiatives that make sense. Continuously raising the bar in terms of performance is not based on pressure from the top, but is an intrinsic aspect of the behaviour of the people in such an organization. This inevitably will lead to successful results that form the basis for positive rewards.

14

Section 9: Deliver results and reward

Deliver results and reward

- Have business results been delivered against targets in at least two out of the last three years?
- Has variable pay (bonuses) at least been at 'par' level on average over the past three years?
- Are results regularly shared with a wider group of people?
- Are people rewarded in other ways, apart from by cash payments?
- Is time in job sufficient to enable a 'delivery culture'?
- Does the organization face brutal facts to learn from past success and failure?

Introduction

In the 1990s, business leaders gave a high level of attention to performance management. The HR function supported this attention by developing various modernized performance management tools. The aim was to attain greater clarity regarding the mutual expectations for the job and the results to be delivered. Overall, higher levels of results and success were sought. Better results were to lead to better rewards. In many cases, reward policies and practices have been modified and updated, to fit with the new performance paradigms. In particular, variable pay or bonus systems were changed to reflect the new reality. Generally speaking, the variable part of the remuneration package has become more important, including share option schemes.

The attitude that young professionals have today with regard to work and career has changed. The 'performance contract' obligations are better understood, but, in turn, the expectations regarding the work that organizations offer today have become more critical. The same applies to the willingness to stay with one organization beyond the current job, which has diminished.

Reward needs to be deserved

We have said that nowadays the 'performance contract' obligations are well understood. This implies that there is awareness that performance and delivery of results cannot be decoupled from reward. In other words, there is no reward without delivery of results.

Despite this, there has probably never been more public debate and challenge about reward issues for top leaders than there is today, and in particular about their bonuses and share option arrangements. The issue seems to be that many people fail to see how the top reward of top leaders can be justified on the basis of their personal contribution and the results they have delivered.

Our assumption is that truly successful leaders who have stayed in their role for a longer period of time, let's say at least five years, will not be questioned about their reward, even if their reward package is very high compared to others'. Jack Welch never had this issue when he was at the helm at General Electric. The reason for this is that he was seen to have personally had a profound impact on GE and that he personally added greatly to the success of GE over a period of many years. Also, he was always loyal to a few very important values, which he applied consistently and fairly in the days when he was the boss at GE. All in all, he delivered recognizable and consistent results against the targets that were set.

The most negative impact has come from cases where new leaders were appointed with reward packages that were perceived as 'exotic', which has caused public upheaval right from the start of their appointment. An example of this occurred when Anders Moberg was appointed early in 2003 as the new CEO for Ahold, the Dutch food company, which was in serious difficulties at the time. It became known that his package included a high bonus that was only partly dependent on results, and a generous leaving package if he were not successful and had to leave the company. He became known as 'the 10 million euro man', even though this number was completely inaccurate. After acrimonious debate, Moberg himself made some concessions to his reward package and announced publicly what these concessions were. After that, the debate calmed down and he could get on with his job.

Have reward levels for top executives gone over the top altogether? In some exceptional situations they may have, but generally speaking we believe that the vast majority of companies and other organizations have responsible reward policies. We are convinced that there is a big challenge for CEOs, reward consultancies and others to explain much better how those policies have been crafted and what can be expected of leaders who have attractive reward packages. The focus should be less on the mechanics and technicalities, although the temptation does exist to give this a lot of attention, since there is an evident lack of basic understanding among most people. Rather, we believe, the focus should be on explaining what key contributions business leaders can make to influence the overall performance and long-term success of the organization. The focus should be on explaining how decisive actions by leaders over time can have a positive impact.

Target setting and aligned (variable) pay practices

The example of Anders Moberg at Ahold shows that if the perception is that there is no clear and understandable link between the reward package (bonus!) and the expected results to be delivered, the reward package starts to work against the new leader and almost prohibits him or her from becoming effective as a leader, energizing the people around him or her and mobilizing the wider workforce. Moberg's decision to make some concessions was a wise one in our view. The materiality of the concessions was not particularly important; what was at stake was whether he would listen to the arguments that were raised and whether he would be willing to make a move to restore his personal credibility. Today the discussion about Moberg's reward package has stopped, and this is surely also because he has shown pretty good leadership in dealing with the profound financial and business issues that Ahold was facing.

In section 4 ('Strategic framework', Chapter 9) we talked about the first necessary step in the process of making a strategic framework intellectually understood, which is to translate it into more tangible and concrete actions. We called this process 'strategy into action'. This process is relevant for clarifying what is expected from an individual in terms of concrete results to be delivered. Thereby, 'strategy into action' can help substantially in arriving at realistic targets to be set for bonus purposes.

One role of HR is to see to it that the 'strategy into action' process is properly organized and understood. Its outcome can be used to define work plans and targets for individuals and teams that are truly aligned with the strategy. Having such plans and targets will support the design of variable pay or bonus systems that are aligned with the strategy. If both the work plans and the variable pay or bonus system are aligned with the strategic framework, this becomes a powerful combination.

Unfortunately, in reality this alignment often does not exist. We would argue that the design or the redesign of the variable pay system should be looked at more actively than is done normally. Basically, every strategic review should be followed by a review of the reward practices, particularly for the variable part of the reward.

Is it impossible, then, to get the process right for creating clear and understandable links between the setting of targets, the delivery of results and variable pay or bonus? Many organizations have been struggling with that process. Despite the putting into place of pretty sophisticated systems, the reality seems to be patchy. There are good examples of how the setting of stretching targets and the following delivery of results led to motivating bonus payments. There are also many examples of situations where things happened in the internal or external world that were not foreseen at the time the targets and the expected delivery of results were set. In those cases the motivation of people was damaged rather than stimulated.

The dissatisfaction with existing variable pay or bonus systems has led to attempts to create even more sophisticated target-setting systems, trying to anticipate any possible change that might occur. Such attempts have as a rule proved to be rather counter-productive. In addition, this approach requires a detailed administration of the target-setting process, its outcome and the determination of the bonuses.

Deliver consistent results over time and (variable) pay

We believe that reward, in particular variable pay, should be based on a track record of consistent delivery of results against targets, rather than on a bureaucratic assessment of short-term results against short-term targets. In our view, the future development of effective, well-understood and sustainable reward policies and systems will need to be done along the following lines:

- Organizations that on the basis of their nature have shown that they can create a consistent cycle of target setting, delivery of results and variable pay (bonus, share options, shares, etc) within a recurring time period of one year should continue to do so. This may be particularly true for some companies at more operational levels, where the results can be measured on a relatively short-term basis. However, we believe that most organizations would be better off if they stretched this cycle to a two- or even three-year period, especially for top management. This would do away with short-termism, which often confuses the process and the outcomes, particularly if the stakes are (very) high. Payout of a bonus or share options could still be done on a yearly basis, but the final assessment how successful a person has been would be made on the basis of a two-year performance period.

- There should be more room for discretion. Schemes with detailed formulas do not lead to better outcomes, since in many cases it is impossible to forecast expected results in ever greater detail. Instead, we suggest that a limited set of key measures be formulated and agreed, and that these be combined with a greater use of discretion. We believe this arrangement will result in better outcomes, although it will only work if there is trust within the organization.

In any organization there will be some values that are of paramount importance and that therefore always need to be lived by an individual member of that organization. If a person does not live up to these values, this should clearly have a negative influence on his or her reward.

4

Future contexts and considerations for business HR

15

Key trends for HR

We are observing a number of developments in the corporate world that are having an impact on HR or will have an impact in the near future. Some of those key trends have already been recognized and have been the basis for reviewing what HR does and how HR is organized.

We will give a brief overview of the trends that we believe are the most relevant ones:

- corporate governance;
- teams;
- HR as contributor to the business;
- international HR competencies required;
- productivity drive;
- the growing importance of private equity;
- HR outsourcing.

Corporate governance

Transparency, or a lack of it, has become a major issue. After some scandals with far-reaching consequences, international initiatives have been taken to increase transparency. Sarbanes–Oxley, the US Act on corporate governance, is a prime example of such an initiative. Other, local initiatives have led to new standards, codes of conduct, further regulation, etc. Transparency is an absolute requirement if a company wants to attract money from financial institutions and investors. Many companies have had to change their corporate governance. In this context we see it as the role of HR to take the lead on integrity issues internally and to ensure that clarity is provided on the role of various governance bodies, their relationships and board (performance) contracts.

Teams

Leadership will shift to team leadership. The time of the 'celebrity CEO' is over. In the recovering economy of recent years, teams with in-depth knowledge of the business are needed to create an effective team climate for innovation. Leadership will enhance diversity in teams to stimulate the effectiveness of teams and to boost innovation.

HR as contributor to the business

In many companies, HR has its seat on the board. It is up to HR to deliver its contribution to the business. High-performing companies have HR executives engaged in the business at strategic level. Businesses have changed, and HR needs to respond to the changes by adding true HR value to the business – a development that will be further strengthened in the coming years. HR executives need to have deep knowledge of the business, just as do other board members. The contribution of HR is about HR issues but will increasingly also be about broader business issues.

International HR competencies required

The business environment has become global. Companies have to adapt to this new situation, and have to adapt fast. Successful economies in Asia seem take a global perspective anyhow. Businesses will need to develop international competencies. HR will need to organize itself internationally and develop international HR competencies. A new balance between the central control of international HR strategies and activities on the one hand and responsiveness to local circumstances on the other needs to be found. New roles are emerging in HR. New competencies are required.

Productivity drive

Companies across the world are under pressure to be more productive. Employee effectiveness and improving productivity are key in the competitive arena. The huge difference between labour costs in the East and those in the West is shifting the impetus of job creation to the East. How can businesses in other parts of the world respond to this and survive? HR will need to be creative about flexible and smart work organizations.

HR outsourcing

Companies need to think through carefully what their business HR priorities are and whether outsourcing should be among the top two or three priorities. Embarking on an outsourcing project will require a major effort of the HR executives and key HR operators over a period of several years. HR outsourcing is the trend, although inspiring examples of completed outsourcing projects are few and far between. Given the importance of this topic for HR, we will have a separate chapter on HR outsourcing (Chapter 17).

The growing importance of private equity

More recently we have seen an increase in the activities of private equity firms. Huge amounts of private equity are available to buy companies and take them from the public sector into the private arena. The companies that are being sold include business units and divisions of large international companies. Private equity is relatively unknown and therefore we have decided to devote a separate chapter to this (Chapter 16). In this chapter we will also look at the role of business HR in managing the transfer from public company to private company.

16

Private equity and business HR: disaster or blessing?

In 2001, private equity firms were responsible for 7 per cent of all European merger and acquisition activity by volume. By 2005 the proportion had gone up to 13 per cent, and a further increase is under way. In 2006, approximately 205 billion euros of capital was committed to private equity firms in Europe alone. As a result of these activities, many businesses have changed ownership. Not only medium-sized stand-alone companies, but also many units and divisions of larger international public companies have moved into the private arena.

We have already referred in an earlier chapter to an interview with Ben Verwaayen, CEO of British Telecom, about the role of HR:

> HR should come out of their comfort zone. They have an important role to play. When they see opportunities to improve the performance of the business by paying more and better attention to the human side of the business, they should speak up and go for it. This takes courage, but HR needs to do it.

This triggers the question how HR can add value in a private equity environment. Private equity firms are not very popular, and some believe that they have no long-term future. For those people it is time for a wake-up call. Private equity firms are here to stay, and this is not necessarily bad for business life. Let's have a closer look at how private equity firms work and then look at the value HR can add.

How private equity works

Private equity firms normally buy majority stakes in companies and expect returns on their investment over a period of three to seven years. They typically fund the purchase of companies through debt and require double-digit return on investment. Participation in a private equity deal offers the management team of an acquired business an entrepreneurial opportunity and more flexibility and freedom – and financial independence in the event that the 'exit' scenario after five years or so is successful. Private equity firms expect management teams to hold an equity stake in the company. Typically the portion of investment required is one to two times the combined base salaries of management.

For the management team, working in a private company implies that there is a more active interaction with the shareholders and the board. Plans are based on a five-year time horizon, rather than one or two years. Private companies can also afford this longer-term focus, given the reduced public scrutiny they work under. If a deviation from the plans occurs, private equity firms say that they are able to correct this faster and more adequately than many large corporations do. This is one of the reasons why private equity firms are able to outpace large public companies. To use a sailing metaphor, they are able to 'sail more to windward'.

For the employees, we expect working for a private company to imply a greater emphasis on performance-related pay and a 'sharper' assessment and selection approach. Performance targets are set as close as possible to the area an individual can influence. Accountability at all levels is reinforced. Normally, terms and conditions are updated and made more flexible. If success does not materialize, this may lead to lower rewards.

Differences between public and private companies

Compared to public companies, the generally positive differences in private companies are as follows:

- *Reduced public scrutiny, allowing longer-term focus.* More and more public companies are frustrated about the increasing demands from financial markets to provide frequent (quarterly) progress reports on company results. Making one mistake can immediately lead to a lower share price. The mounting pressure to hear positive news can lead to unbalanced pressure within corporations. Private companies do not have this pressure and, although the image they have may be different, are able to focus on the execution of their long-term plan.

- *Flexibility and freedom.* Private equity shareholders monitor closely how a business performs, and when corrections may be required, they are not hindered by the conflicting policies and priorities that in many cases slow down decision making in large public companies.

- *An entrepreneurial challenge.* Businesses acquired by private equity firms normally do not change ownership because they were highly successful in the eyes of the previous owner, rightly or wrongly. Therefore, the change to private company status is normally seen as an opportunity to do things differently and better.

- *Higher potential rewards.* In the approach that private equity firms take, the rewards play an important role. The upside potential for those who acquire equity in the new company is normally very attractive, and this is what seems to have a major impact. Many people who have made the change from a public to a private company describe this factor as the key driver of different behaviour and a different culture.

The differences generally seen as negative in private companies as compared with public companies are as follows:

- *Higher risk.* Not all private companies work out successfully. The downside of potential higher rewards is potential lower rewards and loss of equity in the event of failure.

- *Greater focus on financial aspects.* In their monitoring of private companies, detailed financial management is applied by the new owners. High debt ratios have to be managed, and in everything the company does, financial considerations will always be at the forefront.

This is not to say that this is not the case in public companies, but in public companies other considerations may also play a larger role.

● *Potential for consolidation.* At the time of acquisition, private equity firms are already considering exit scenarios for the acquired company in some four, five or six years' time. Given the fact that many private companies are medium-sized, it is not impossible that they will eventually be consolidated with larger entities (again).

Adding value through HR

As we have said, the expectations to perform are quite high for an acquired company. Private equity firms are aware that the human factor is one of the key factors for success. They will want to assess properly the human capabilities for successful and sustainable value creation before a company is acquired. And after acquisition they will want the acquired company to become really high-performing. For both they need business HR professionals to focus on the relationship between business strategy, organization and people. Our belief is that it will only be a matter of time before private equity firms have business HR professionals on their teams.

There is a huge challenge for HR executives and professionals currently working in companies that may be acquired by private equity in future. Do they dare to stick their neck out? Do they have the courage to present plans to the new owner that will indeed create more value? Is there potential on the human side of acquired businesses to perform better under new ownership?

HR in general should in our view start to work on this sort of challenge long before private equity comes around. These are things that make business HR jobs exciting. As Ben Verwaayen said, 'When HR sees opportunities to improve the performance of the business by paying more and better attention to the human side of the business, they should speak up and go for it. This takes courage, but HR needs to do it.'

17

HR outsourcing

British Telecom (BT) is among a number of large companies that decided to outsource a considerable part of their HR activities some years ago. The contract covers more than 120,000 employees, thousands of contractors and more than 300,000 pensioners. The outsourced activities include the admin tasks for payroll, benefits administration, etc, but also cover parts of the resourcing process, performance management process and learning process.

Like BT, other large corporations have sought to outsource part of their HR activities in recent years. Outsourcing has become increasingly popular. Not all recent outsourcing projects have been hugely successful, however. In not all cases have the high expectations, especially regarding cost reductions, been met. In some cases, projects have been scaled down after a large-scale start.

We have argued that companies need to think through carefully what their business HR priorities are and whether outsourcing should be among the top two or three priorities at a certain point in time. What is certain is that embarking on an outsourcing project will require a major effort on the part of the HR executives and key HR operators over a period of several years.

In order to gain more clarity as to what the main considerations are regarding the decision to outsource HR tasks to a third-party service provider, we want to look in a little more detail at what the main drivers for outsourcing are, what the key pros and cons are and what the associated risks are.

Main drivers of outsourcing

The main driver for HR managers seems to be an improvement and upgrading of the HR service. They do acknowledge that cost reduction is important as well, but their main consideration is that they want to make more time available for so-called strategic HR activities by outsourcing the time-consuming matters of daily routine. Doing so will allow them to add more value to the business they work for.

Top management seems to be primarily interested in cost reduction through the outsourcing of HR activities. Top managers also see outsourcing as a way to avoid large investments in technology for HR service purposes. Service improvement is relevant for top managers, but it does not feature among the top three considerations for outsourcing.

It is important to note that the expectations of top management and HR management may well differ. Potentially this could lead to a situation whereby HR is struggling to deliver the expected cost savings by top management, while not being able to give form and shape to the more strategic role that HR wants to play as a partner in business. In an extreme form this could lead to a situation whereby the added value from HR eventually is only coming from the cost reduction it is able to achieve in its own functional organization. The way to avoid this dilemma is to be very clear in the business case for an outsourcing project about the specific cost savings to be expected and to provide a similar degree of clarity about the expected future strategic HR contribution.

With regard to expected cost reductions, these depend greatly on where a company is 'coming from'. On the one hand, if a company has already made substantial investments in standardizing HR processes and systems across functions, geographical locations, etc, the assessment may be that the use of an external outsourcing firm will lead only to modest cost reductions. In this situation the argument may also be used that the company does not want to say goodbye to employees with critical functional knowledge. The company may not want to see these brains leave the company with outsourcing.

On the other hand, if a company has not invested properly in leveraging HR processes and systems across functions, geographical locations, etc, the potential cost reduction in an outsourcing scenario may be very attractive. In this situation the availability of a single service provider for outsourced HR tasks will play an important role. A new dilemma may occur in this scenario, which is that the cost of conversion from the current situation to an outsourced future potentially can be very high.

Key pros and cons of outsourcing

Let us start with the main perceived **advantages** of outsourcing of HR tasks. One of the most frequently used arguments in favour of outsourcing is that third-party providers are in a better position to deliver outsourced HR services, given the fact that this is their core business. Because it is their core business, the service providers will pay more attention to creating an efficient organization with the right sort of people and skills. They need to make money from their business and need to do all the sorts of things other profit organizations do to be successful.

The second 'pro' is related to the first. Third-party service providers operating in this manner will need to invest in state-of-the-art technology to support the activities for their clients. In other words, they invest in this instead of each of the clients doing it themselves on a smaller scale.

Third, the outsourcing of HR tasks is the lowest-cost scenario compared to other scenarios. The scale advantage allows outside service providers to operate at more competitive cost levels.

And finally, connected with this is the fact that risks are moved from the company itself to the third-party service provider.

The main perceived **disadvantages** of outsourcing of HR tasks are the following.

PART FOUR

First, the company becomes dependent for the effective delivery of part of its overall HR services on a third-party provider. Contracts with those service providers tend be for several years (at least five) and require large sums of money to be paid.

Second, HR outsourcing projects require that relatively (very) high numbers of HR employees are made redundant. Our experience is that the minimum number of employees to be made redundant is in the region of 20–25 per cent and the maximum can be as high as 50 per cent of the existing HR establishment. One has to think through carefully what message the decision to outsource big parts of the HR workforce sends out to the whole organization, not just the HR side of it.

Third, the conversion from internally managed HR services to an outsourcing scenario is complex and time-consuming. If not managed properly, the transition could lead to a breakdown in the delivery of existing services, which will be expensive to remedy and will have a negative impact on employees' morale.

And finally, there is the question of whether the users of HR services, the internal clients of HR, will be able to adapt to the new way of working. Line managers and employees at various levels will need to be informed about the HR services that they can expect and, more importantly, that they should not expect. The worst situation occurs if the new order comes into force while parts of the organization continue to work in the old manner.

The above overview of pros and cons is certainly not exhaustive, but it touches on a number of topics that need to be looked at carefully and that need to be discussed in detail before an organization decides to outsource HR tasks.

Managing the risks of HR outsourcing

We have already mentioned a number of risks. We believe that the greatest risk is to create unrealistic expectations regarding cost reduction. HR will shoot itself in the foot if this is allowed to happen. The way to avoid over-expectations is, in our view, to take proper time for the preparation of an outsourcing project. This time should be used to make a detailed and robust plan for the activities to be outsourced and to discuss the key elements of this plan as early as possible with the key stakeholders.

The second biggest risk we see is that the HR team underestimates the amount of effort required for the outsourcing project itself and commits itself to an HR agenda on which outsourcing is only one of various other HR priorities to be delivered to the business. Normally this will be impossible to do. Therefore, it will be required to rearrange the HR agenda with the key stakeholders in the organization and to reduce the number of HR priorities other than HR outsourcing to only a very few other key HR contributions. If, given the business situation, there is an urgent need to work on additional priorities, HR will have to give a clear picture of the extra resources that it will require to manage both the HR outsourcing project and the other HR priorities.

Another important risk lies in the fact that between 20 per cent and 50 per cent of the existing HR workforce will lose their job as a result of HR outsourcing. For the HR function itself, a detailed change agenda will need to be prepared to manage resistance to change. This issue certainly needs to be managed carefully within the HR function, but it may affect the climate and morale in the wider organization too. There is no 'one size fits all' solution for this, but everything we have said about compelling communication so far should be used to mitigate the risks of creating a low morale.

One final comment. Outsourcing is not easy. Good planning is key. Clarity on expected cost reduction is vital to avoid the perception later in the project that HR is lousy in delivering the benefits. Fundamental changes will occur in HR itself, but the success of the project is also dependent on how others adapt to the new situation. There are many risks, but most of them can be managed in one way or another. However, if the culture of the organization goes against outsourcing, much more time will be needed before any decision on outsourcing is made. This could be the case in companies where existing HR services are to a large extent perceived to drive the culture of the organization and the good relations with employees in different geographical locations.

PART FOUR

18

The creation of HR value in different sectors

The respondents to the checklist used for the bulk of this book's research work in a broad range of different sectors, and this triggers the question of whether the HR priorities in the chemicals sector are significantly different from those in the pharmaceutical industry. We have used Hay Group's extensive experience with many sectors and industries in recent years to give an impression of the HR activities that seem to be found important and that seem to add HR value. We provide an overview for each of the following 13 sectors:

- chemicals;
- consumer products;
- education;
- finance;
- healthcare;
- manufacturing;
- oil and gas;
- pharmaceuticals;

- the public sector;

- retail;

- technology;

- telecommunications;

- utilities.

We advise you to select the sector(s) that are relevant to you and to go to that specific part of this chapter.

Chemicals

The chemicals industry worldwide faces many and varied pressures as its key players strive to maintain consistent growth and profitability. Not least among these pressures is the steadily increasing price of petroleum products, which has dealt a double blow to the chemicals sector, as these products are both the raw materials for much of its output and a vital source of fuel.

Another pressure facing the sector is the intensifying focus on environmental issues, as governments and lobbyists around the world step up efforts to address climate change and consumers demand 'greener' solutions to their everyday needs.

The chemicals industry is also confronted with particular human resources issues, namely a legacy of high wages and an ageing employee population, especially in Western countries. These factors place upward pressure on costs, and have led some analysts to predict a slowing in the talent pipeline for the near future.

In addition, universal industry trends such as greater competition, relentless globalization and ongoing consolidation are converging to make succeeding in this sector a continuing challenge. One of the challenges for the world's leading chemical companies is to manage the industry's cycles and pressures more effectively through improved human resources management.

Some of the HR issues that chemical companies have spent considerable time on include the following:

- Clarifying *role accountability* and *performance expectations* – especially in increasingly matrixed, global organizational structures.
- Developing the *calibre of leadership* required to lead and manage change in a highly technical industry.
- Developing the *talent pipeline* needed to meet future needs and ensure smooth succession at all levels in the future.
- Developing *total remuneration programmes* to ensure alignment of reward with business strategy and the sector's complex global structures. Benchmarking best practice within the industry and across global organizations.
- Measuring and managing *employee attitudes* through detailed staff surveys, which enable chemical companies to manage change more effectively.

Consumer products

As if providing food, beverages, tobacco, household goods and personal care products to consumers in every corner of the globe were not a complex enough business, the fast-moving consumer goods (FMCG) sector faces its own particular challenges. FMCG companies must strive to balance the needs of local consumers in culturally diverse markets with the need to develop powerful global brands to attract and retain the loyalty of consumers. At the same time, lasting and mutually beneficial partnerships with retailers are essential to deliver these products to the consumer at a margin that is acceptable to both parties.

The sector must also manage innovation effectively, to ensure a pipeline of high-quality products for the future to help maintain an edge over generic brands.

As the industry becomes increasingly global in order to manage the least cost–best price business model, the international nature of the industry poses further, equally intense challenges:

- Developing efficient, effective supply chains.

- Striking the balance between centralized management and local flexibility.

- Instilling a global organizational culture and mindset.

- Taking advantage of opportunities to grow and rationalize brands through mergers, acquisitions, and disposals.

To stay at the forefront of the sector's efforts to meet these challenges, food, beverage, tobacco, household goods and personal care companies have done extensive work on issues such as the following:

- *Organizational transformation* – restructuring and organizing to manage growth.
- *Cultural change* – developing global mindsets and growth-oriented cultures.
- *Leadership transformation* – developing the leadership required to ensure growth and lead complex global organizations while meeting local market needs.
- *Performance management* – designing performance frameworks that combine a focus on results and accountability with employee development.
- *Brand talent* – creating competency frameworks to enable the identification and development of the best brand leaders.
- *Sales force development* – improving the performance and motivation of global sales forces.
- *Reward planning* – providing policies and frameworks for remuneration of all employees.

Education

Education providers are under severe pressure from a range of stakeholders with diverse and often heartfelt interests: central and local government, teachers, parents and employers, not to mention the wider public.

For many years, reforming and improving education in the primary, secondary and tertiary sectors has been a number one priority for governments all over the world, and public- and private-sector providers are coming under more scrutiny than ever before.

Further education providers are facing an enormous explosion in demand at a time when government funding is increasingly constrained. The sector is exploring new business models such as mixed private-/public-sector educational provision. Meanwhile, students are becoming more international in their choice of universities and colleges, forcing providers to respond to competition by enhancing quality and benchmarking qualifications to international standards.

In the primary and secondary sectors, pressure is equally intense, as calls from politicians and parents for higher standards leads to greater government involvement in all aspects of education. This imposes greater burdens on head teachers, who are taking on new management responsibilities for finance and introducing government-led change.

Public- and private-sector schools of all kinds range from high-performance establishments to 'turnaround' schools facing deep-rooted challenges. Developing resilient leaders is essential for effective education providers.

Key activities undertaken in educational establishments include the following:

- *Mergers* – integrating universities to manage all aspects of the structural, process and cultural changes involved in a complex merger.
- *Leadership development* – education professionals at all levels (teachers, head teachers, lecturers and researchers) becoming world-class leaders.
- *Remuneration* – ensuring that education institutions remain competitive in developing, motivating and retaining both academic and support staff.

Finance

The unremitting change that has affected the financial services industry in recent years shows no sign of abating. Compliance has become the industry watchword over the past decade, following a spate of high-profile collapses. Sarbanes–Oxley and similar legislation has placed enormous pressure on financial services firms not only to comply with immensely complicated rules and regulations, but to provide faultless transparency as they do so. This pressure for compliance, while imposed by governments, also comes from shareholders and customers, many of whom are also demanding a more ethical approach to investment decisions.

Aside from regulatory compliance, the challenges that have faced financial markets are many and fundamental, including major deregulation, relentless globalization, intensifying competition and steadily declining customer loyalty.

Key activities in the financial services industry addressing these issues include the following:

- *Organizational change and restructuring* – transforming finance companies' organizational structures, leaving them better placed to face the opportunities and threats posed by a rapidly evolving market.
- *Customer service* – making call centre management more effective and improving the capabilities of the people managing and working in call centres.
- *Leadership transformation* – deepening organizations' understanding of the leadership capabilities required to make their companies market leaders, and implementing programmes to develop these attributes.
- *Talent development* – creating talent and career development processes to enable companies to nurture talent for the challenges of the future as well as the present.

- *Ethics* – addressing the challenge of operating in a way that is both performance oriented and ethical at the same time – a critical pressure in the current industry climate.
- *Remuneration* – having the right remuneration strategies to link remuneration to performance, and satisfying the need for employee motivation in a way that will stand up to scrutiny from the public and shareholders alike.
- *Role evaluation* – organizations needing to understand the huge changes the industry is experiencing, and their impact on role accountability and career development.

Healthcare

Healthcare provision the world over is facing enormous change – change that is affecting both public- and private-sector providers in equal measure. In many countries the pressure for change is leading to the emergence of totally new business models and management strategies for healthcare provision.

This evolution is triggered by a range of factors, from the growing demand for healthcare by an ageing population to the increasing costs of high-tech medicines and equipment, and the growing expectations among patients for a better and faster service. All this change impacts on the healthcare sector at a time when there are huge pressures on finances, whether from private health insurance or from state funding. Healthcare managers must increasingly balance the conflicting priorities of greater medical excellence and patient service with ever-tighter budgets.

Hence, radical new business and management models are emerging to enable healthcare provision to develop in line with patient expectations: public-/private-sector collaboration is on the increase and healthcare providers are having to balance greater managerial control over resources. New structures for balancing corporate governance and regulatory compliance with stakeholder demands are being developed. All this is taking place in a sector traditionally run by specialized clinicians seeking to provide the best care for their particular patients.

Key activities for healthcare providers to master the challenges they are facing are as follows:

- *Organizational transformation* – providers managing the conflicting priorities they face and developing business and management models to improve efficiency and effectiveness. Turning healthcare organizations' strategies into reality by creating the structures and processes required to implement necessary changes.
- *Leadership transformation* – identifying the talent needed to lead in times of change. Developing leaders who understand and can manage complex change, while maintaining and enhancing team effectiveness.
- *Employee development* – enabling employees to develop the skills and behavioural attributes required to adjust to change and thrive in a new and ever-evolving climate.
- *Diversity* – generating diversity programmes to empower all healthcare employees, irrespective of background, to develop their capabilities and draw on their full potential.
- *Remuneration* – ensuring that employees at all levels are fairly rewarded for their responsibility and performance, as benchmarked against the wider market.
- *Employee attitudes* – understanding employees' attitudes, to better support them through the process of change.

Manufacturing

Manufacturing is an industry that has faced overwhelming challenges for a number of decades, particularly in the industrialized world, where firms are under pressure from developing countries. The onslaught of competition from so-called tiger economies, which benefit from significantly lower cost bases, is making even day-to-day survival a critical issue for many manufacturers in the West. Heavy price competition and rising commodity prices have eroded profit margins.

The pressures on manufacturing companies to globalize, to outsource production to the most cost-efficient offshore locations, to embrace the cost savings offered by new technologies, to improve quality, to achieve greater flexibility of output and to respond to rapidly changing customer needs – all pose enormous and complex challenges, not the least being the relentless downward pressure on costs.

Supply chains are growing ever longer, requiring more sophisticated and increasingly complicated logistics. Procurement is being transformed by web-based technologies. Energy prices are augmenting costs.

Key activities for manufacturing include the following:

- *Organizational structure* – developing organizations capable of managing global production effectively.
- *Role design* – designing accountable and performance-focused roles.
- *Managing remuneration* – aligning pay programmes (especially variable pay) more accurately with costs. In the West there is relentless pressure on 'people' costs – such as compensation and healthcare benefits.
- *Team effectiveness* – developing team-based structures for organizations, a critical attribute in manufacturing.
- *Leadership transformation* – developing the capabilities needed to lead in an industry undergoing huge pressures, challenges and change.
- *Employee attitudes* – enabling manufacturers to understand employee attitudes and concerns, in order to create HR programmes and policies that will lead to the greatest returns in terms of employee motivation.

Oil and gas

The oil and gas industry, though widely reported to be riding high on elevated levels of profitability as the price of crude goes up, still faces stiff challenges. Most crucial among the pressures weighing on the industry is the unceasing search to secure the future of its very lifeblood, namely the need to access vital future oil reserves.

While exploration continues, other day-to-day pressures exist: the drive to extract greater quantities from existing wells; and managing the competitiveness of downstream retail activities, as the forecourts face price competition from 'conventional' retailers such as supermarkets.

Oil companies also face enormous environmental challenges in the form of opposition from a vocal and increasingly influential environmental lobby, whose voice is heeded more and more by consumers. The environmental challenge is exacerbated by continuous threats from government in the form of increased taxation.

The industry is by its nature a highly globalized one, with the result that events in any one territory, such as hurricanes in the Caribbean, can have a huge impact upon oil availability and prices the world over.

Key activities in oil and gas include the following:

- *Organizational restructuring* – addressing critical strategic questions such as whether companies' structures are optimally organized to achieve their objectives.
- *Leadership development* – defining the leadership capabilities needed to succeed in the sector's highly competitive and complex environment.
- *Employee attitudes* – understanding the attitudes and concerns of employees in order to define more motivational HR policies.
- *Talent development* – identifying the talent needed and introducing career development programmes to develop talent to its full potential.
- *Reward management/grading* – job grading and reward strategy.

Pharmaceuticals

Globally, the pharmaceuticals industry is undergoing fundamental change. Regulatory demands, product issues, pricing pressures, the growth of managed care and the ongoing challenges of innovation and consolidation are all major issues that pharmaceutical companies face.

The industry is also under increasing pressure to shorten product life cycles and get new drugs to market more quickly and efficiently. Investors are growing impatient with the decade or longer it can take to develop a major new drug and the short window of opportunity to make a return on their investment.

Pharmaceuticals is a knowledge-based industry, whose primary challenge is managing innovation. However, many pharmaceutical companies are extremely large and lack the agility to complete major undertakings quickly – two counter-productive traits when it comes to speeding up market cycles.

Pharmaceutical companies have to manage both product development and sales, fusing geographical and functional lines, and so need integrated but matrixed structures to share knowledge and implement new strategies seamlessly. The key issue is: how do organizations quicken product development cycles and reduce human capital costs, while producing sound sales targeting and effective clinical trials? This is a difficult and expensive balancing act.

The pharmaceutical industry is moving from the 'blockbuster drug' model to developing products that are more targeted and focused, which needs a very different approach whereby huge revenues from one or two products are replaced with specialist drugs that produce more incremental income streams.

And, of course, all pharmaceutical companies face the cost and effectiveness issues of gaining greater sales performance – how to ensure that clinicians choose their products, and retail customers buy their over-the-counter offerings.

PART FOUR

Key activities that have been undertaken within the global pharmaceutical industry include the following:

- *Leadership transformation* – developing the leaders required to steer companies through the volatile changes the sector is facing.
- *Sales force effectiveness* – developing leading-edge diagnostics and development processes, helping organizations to develop more effective sales forces.
- *Organizational design* – developing the organizational structures best suited to the challenges facing the industry.
- *Team effectiveness* – seeking to enable employees at all levels to work successfully in highly matrixed organizations.
- *Employee attitudes* – researching employees' attitudes and developing programmes to prioritize motivation.
- *Remuneration* – developing fair and competitive remuneration policies that reward accountability and performance.

The public sector

The one constant in the public sector is the need for change. The public sector never sits still. Initiatives are continually being recommended, and fundamental reform programmes are constantly being implemented to achieve ever better results.

Every week around the world, laws are passed, fresh challenges are set and new issues emerge. In industrialized nations and the developing world, every civil servant is working to improve the *status quo.*

The same pressure for change exists at local government level. Local authorities are often the subject of central government-led change, and are where change in some countries has been greatest, with the privatization of many public services.

Change needs to be approached through both an organization's structure and its people. Is the organization structured to support a change initiative? Have the right roles been defined in order to implement the desired change? Do the people in those roles have the right skills to achieve that change?

Key activities undertaken in the public sector include the following:

- *Organizational effectiveness* – executive teams addressing the overall effectiveness and performance of their organization. Exploring the issues facing public bodies from a holistic perspective and analysing structures to ensure that they support new or existing strategic goals.
- *'Leadership Transformation'* – developing leaders and helping them understand the impact they have on the people and culture they lead; this has been proved to enhance performance. Understanding the skills needed for individuals to excel in their roles ensures that leaders and their organizations can benefit from high-performance teams.
- *'Reward Strategies' Remuneration* – designing reward strategies aligned to organizational goals, government strategy and employees' motivations.
- *'Employee & Customer Surveys' Employee attitudes* – managing change through better understanding of employee concerns and motivations.

Retail

No other industry runs at quite the same fast and relentless pace as retail. The need to keep the finger on the consumer pulse, the hourly measurement of sales and the rapid evolution of product portfolios mean that retail is truly the industry that never sleeps.

To heighten the challenge, the retailer's ability to meet the demands of increasingly selective and cost-conscious consumers is being eroded by the highly complex forces affecting the industry. Increasing globalization in a traditionally national business – with the continuing expansion of global giants such as Wal-Mart, Tesco, Carrefour – and ongoing diversification along both market and product lines are constantly changing the rules of the retail game.

PART FOUR

The need to maintain low prices and high margins places extreme pressure on the costs that can be paid to suppliers and the wages that can be paid to staff. Meanwhile, retailers must differentiate themselves on product quality and service provision.

The following activities have been undertaken by leading retailers to enhance crucial aspects of their business:

- *Organizational effectiveness* – creating structures that enable retailers to compete successfully and react nimbly to constant change.
- *Leadership transformation* – developing the leadership teams required to manage global firms operating in a highly complex, rapidly moving market.
- *People strategies* – designing programmes to enhance talent development and employee motivation at all levels of retail organizations.
- *Remuneration* – developing remuneration strategies and structures for all levels of employees from the shop floor to senior executives, balancing the need for employee motivation and the cost-effectiveness demanded by shareholder and public scrutiny.
- *Employee engagement* – surveying employee attitudes to better understand employee motivation, and delivering programmes to enhance employee engagement.

Technology

The global technology sector – embracing software, hardware and IT services – has been one of the boom industries of the past decade. The pace of technological development has been phenomenal, driving not only growth but new product and service convergences.

The sector has also seen more changes in business models than most: globalization, consolidation, outsourcing, offshoring – the sector leads the world in the scale and pace of change. And, as the current IT boom in India illustrates, the technology sector has the power to improve entire economies.

For managers in the sector, the pace of technological innovation and organizational change bring particular demands: the need to maintain deep understanding of ever-changing technology; the ability to capitalize on technological advances to create new products and services to meet evolving customer needs; the skills to manage the risks involved in major investments; and building scale through mergers and acquisitions – the list is endless.

Key activities in the technology industry include the following:

- *Leadership assessment and development* – senior managers developing the leadership skills required to be successful in a global environment.
- *Organizational restructuring* – creating effective and accountable organizations.
- *Remuneration management* – maximizing the value of organizations' reward budget by aligning performance and pay.

Telecommunications

The telecommunications industry and the services it provides have changed beyond recognition in the past decade. Telecom organizations have transformed their business operations from being national monopolies to being lean global competitors, adapted for growth *and* customer retention, and have changed their core business from the provision of fixed-line services to converged voice and data provision across fixed and mobile platforms.

The key challenge facing today's telecoms remains the drive to stay ahead in an industry whose core offering is constantly adapting to deliver the latest technology to global business and consumers alike. Large-scale restructuring and multiple changes of ownership have presented challenges for companies seeking to organize and motivate their people to deliver. Increased consolidation in the sector and organizational complexity has to be combined with the agility required to succeed in a fast-evolving market.

And yet more challenges lie ahead. Many companies are struggling to strike the balance between growth and customer retention. In saturated Western markets, product differentiation, service and innovation are key; at the same time, there is the rush for market share in less developed regions, which pose their own cultural challenges.

Key activities in the telecommunications industry include the following:

- *Employee motivation and engagement* – understanding how to engage and motivate people in order to improve performance.
- *Leadership assessment and development* – developing leadership capabilities, ensuring that managers have the skills to deliver complex business strategies.
- *Reward management* – maximizing the value of organizations' reward budget by aligning performance and pay.
- *Organizational restructuring* – creating effective and accountable organizations.

Utilities

Today's utility companies face an era of rapid and fundamental change. Both public- and private-sector providers must respond to a constantly changing regulatory framework and operate in a market structured along increasingly global lines. The nature of utilities organizations is evolving, with deregulation, privatization and consolidation making change the only constant in this industry.

Energy providers also face the additional burden of relentless cost pressures from dramatically rising fuel costs. Against this backdrop, customers are demanding better, cheaper services delivered with minimum environmental impact.

The structure of the utilities industry varies greatly from country to country, along with the pattern of ownership and regulation.

Some examples of activities undertaken by utility companies include the following:

- *Organizational transformation* – adapting to profound change, such as privatization, mergers and acquisitions. For example, power companies developing organizational structures and performance models fit for an ever-changing market.
- *Change management* – managing change effectively. For instance, focusing leadership teams on the areas of accountability that will deliver the greatest success in the new environment, and delivering programmes to support workforces in adapting to the changing demands of new business models.
- *Performance management* – creating accountable organizations based on clear performance metrics. This includes building in the development processes required to encourage employees to achieve better results now and in the future.
- *Leadership development* – senior managers enhancing the leadership capabilities they need to steer their organizations through fundamental organizational change.
- *Talent management* – creating talent management processes for utility companies to identify, retain and develop world-class talent.
- *Employee attitudes* – designing and conducting employee surveys to deepen organizations' understanding of their staff's priorities and concerns, which in turn enables management to develop employee engagement and motivation programmes to increase productivity and satisfaction.
- *Rewards* – designing competitive total remuneration programmes that reinforce providers' focus on accountability and performance, comply with regulations and are acceptable to all stakeholders.

Index

ALSO AVAILABLE FROM KOGAN PAGE

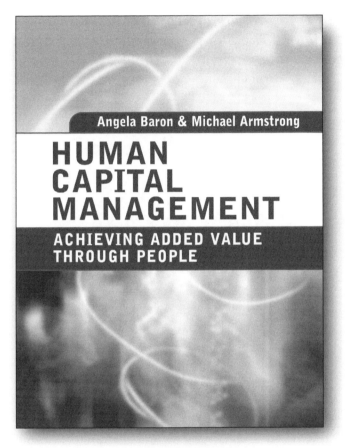

Angela Baron & Michael Armstrong

HUMAN CAPITAL MANAGEMENT

ACHIEVING ADDED VALUE THROUGH PEOPLE

ISBN 13: 978 0 7494 4938 4
ISBN 10: 0 7494 4938 1
Hardback   2007

ALSO AVAILABLE FROM KOGAN PAGE

"The virtues of this book are its lucidity and practical approach. Gobillot sets out a road map for leaders who want to reject formality in favour of seeing what is really happening... The sharp sassy style and a sense of realism ultimately keeps this book on track."
Training and Coaching Today

ISBN 13: 978 0 7494 4830 1
ISBN 10: 0 7494 4830 X
Hardback   2006

ALSO AVAILABLE FROM KOGAN PAGE